CROSSROADS
The Drama of a Soap Opera

Meg's farewell – Noele's goodbye.

CROSSROADS

The Drama of a Soap Opera

Dorothy Hobson

METHUEN

First published in 1982 by
Methuen London Ltd
11 New Fetter Lane, London EC4P 4EE
Copyright © Dorothy Hobson 1982
Printed in Great Britain by
Richard Clay (The Chaucer Press) Ltd
Bungay, Suffolk

British Library Cataloguing in Publication Data
Hobson, Dorothy
    Crossroads.
        1. Crossroads (Television program)
        I. Title
    791.45'72   PN1992.77.C/
    ISBN 0-413-50140-X
    ISBN 0-413-50150-7 Pbk

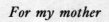
For my mother

Contents

Acknowledgements

I would like to thank everyone at ATV/Central Independent Television who talked to me and allowed me to watch them working, and contributed greatly to the information contained in this book. I am particularly grateful to Charles Denton, who allowed me access to the company in the first place and has remained helpful and supportive throughout the project; also to Jack Barton, who spent a lot of time with me, gave me valuable information and assisted in every way, during what was a difficult time for his own work; and Mike Holgate, who let me watch him work and then had numerous discussions with me about the programme, out of which many ideas developed.

Many people have helped in many different ways and while apologizing in advance for inevitable omissions, I would like to thank the following: Ronald Allen, BBC Archives Department, the Crossroads cast and office staff, the Centre for Contemporary Cultural Studies, Tony Chance, David Cox, David Dunn, Maggie French, David Glencross, Noele Gordon, Neil Grant, Christine Griffin, Stuart Hall, Paul Henry, Mike Hollingsworth, IBA, Ivor Jay, Carolyn Jones, Clem Lewis, Elsbeth Lindner, Peter Ling, Sue Lloyd, Rab McWilliam, Lynette McMorrough, David Moran, Dave Morley, Clare Mulholland, Roger Pearce, Roy Peters, David Reid, Jane Rossington, Jill Sherwin, Norman Smith, Kathy Staff, Graham Walker, Paul Willis, Sue Winder, Harold Wolfenden, Pamela Vezey. Acknowledgement is made to the *Birmingham Evening Mail* for permission to quote from their readers' letters, and to Central Independent Television plc for permission to quote from scripts, which are their copyright.

Deirdre Barker typed the manuscript and transcribed most of the interview tapes, and Mary Ballard and Ann Lane transcribed the remaining tapes. I am particularly grateful to all the women and their families with whom I watched the programme, and the Crossroads viewers who wrote to the *Birmingham Evening Mail*.

Finally, my love and thanks to my own family, Gordon and Mike, for all their help and support.

Introduction

The research for this book began as a small part of a study which I am making for a PhD thesis concerned with the production of popular television programmes and the understanding or appeal of those programmes for their audience. Crossroads, produced at the ATV studios in Birmingham a few miles from my home, had been the first programme which I had wanted to look at three years earlier when I began the project, because it had been identified as a favourite programme by women to whom I had been talking about their television viewing. In the event, it was not until the late spring of 1981 that I managed to gain access to Crossroads, and the period when I was watching the production and viewing with the audience coincided with the period before Noele Gordon was sacked from the company. By the time that the news was announced on Monday 22 June, I had moved on to the news department of ATV, to look at the regional news programme ATV Today, and was able to see the reaction of others in the company to the events. The events of the week from 22 to 27 June and the public outcry of support for the actress and media coverage of those events seemed much more relevant to a book of wider appeal than to remain part of an academic thesis.

Spending time watching people at their jobs is a delicate operation. Initially it is necessary to get to know them and to give them time to decide whether they accept your 'being around' and talking to them about their work. To a certain extent they have the power to resist your intrusion into their working lives or to assist in the work you are trying to do. It is certainly within their power to make your stay a difficult chore or a pleasant and valuable experience. Many of those involved in the programme really had nothing to gain from helping me and potentially they had much to lose. Outsiders studying a work process and questioning those engaged in their daily occupation are always a potential threat – what will they eventually write or say about you? And will there be any repercussions from their findings? There was a second problem in this respect because I had begun the research for an academic project and changed the use of the findings after half the research had been completed. Anyone could have objected to my using what they had told me in this book. My time at Crossroads and the ATV/Central studios has been extremely pleasant. Everyone within the company spoke openly to me and trusted that I would respect their own work situations when I wrote the book. No one asked me not to repeat what they had told me and they gave me complete discretion how I reported and used their words. In fact, no one at ATV/Central has read any of this book and I am grateful for their co-operation and trust.

I have chosen to credit extracts to their speaker as often as I could since the value and relevance of much of what they say is determined by what their role is in the production of the programme. If, however, there were the slightest possibility of repercussions for the speaker I have not used their names. This means that some of the most interesting and certainly the more controversial comments are not credited to their speakers. Also many of my own ideas have been crystallized after talks and discussions with those involved in making the programme at all levels.

This book is as much about the television audience as it is about the programme-makers. The intrusion into the lives of the women and their families, at a time when they were extremely busy, was crucial if I were to be able to understand the viewing of a television programme like Crossroads. There was also the necessity to establish a friendly relationship and to be accepted by the viewers. Often I had talked to the families about other television programmes in the course of the overall research project and it is only by long and relaxed talks and viewing *with* the audience that any understanding of how people watch television can be achieved. The effort is well worth while for it reveals the important contribution which the viewers make to any television programme which they watch.

CHAPTER 1

Real-Life Drama

There's been real-life drama down the road today at ATV studios where Crossroads is made.

BBC Television Midlands Evening News

Soap operas are either loved or hated – they are rarely ignored. Almost anything which happens involving the actors and actresses who play in soap operas is newsworthy, whether it is in the programme or in their own lives. Nothing demonstrated this more than the overwhelming response to and media coverage of the unexpected sacking of the central character in Crossroads in the summer of 1981.

What appears as a small, insignificant event, although personally important to the actress, was orchestrated by the press and television into a major news story. Its significance and news value is in the importance of the soap opera Crossroads and its relationship with the broadcasting institutions, the press and the television audience. The programme is extremely popular yet consistently undervalued and attacked by its critics, and the coverage of the sacking of the actress and the viewers' response to that action provide an illustration of the dichotomy of values held about popular television.

On Monday 22 June, the British public awoke to a startling 'Exclusive' revelation in the *Daily Mirror*, that Noele Gordon had been sacked. The story by Clifford Davis ran:

Actress Noele Gordon has been sacked from her star TV role as Meg Mortimer in Crossroads.

She will leave the cast of the hit soap opera at the end of the year.

Noele said last night, 'I am stunned with sorrow. I'm too upset to discuss the matter. But it is true I have been sacked.'

During the rest of the day the story gathered momentum as radio stations both local and national ran the story in their news bulletins, and by the early evening television news bulletins also carried the story. The Midland commercial television company, ATV, in the guise of its director of programmes, Charles Denton, had decided not to renew the actress's contract and he had issued a special press release to this effect:

MISS NOELE GORDON
Everyone at ATV recognizes the enormous contribution which Noele Gordon has made to ITV over many years. We are also deeply conscious of the affection in which the public holds Meg Mortimer. For the last seventeen years Noele Gordon in the role of Meg Mortimer has been one of Britain's best-loved characters, and a personal friend to millions of viewers. But nothing – particularly in television – can stay unchanged for ever. Our new plans for Crossroads sadly mean that Meg must leave the motel.

For me, personally, this is a sad moment. I have always held Noele Gordon in the highest esteem, both as a television personality and a colleague.
Charles Denton
Director of Programmes

This action earned Charles Denton the undying hate of Crossroads fans, and the national press added fuel to their fury by acting with supportive outrage during the next few days. On Tuesday 23 June, the national tabloids reported the events at the rehearsal rooms when Noele Gordon had arrived on Monday morning. According to the *Daily Mirror*, she arrived 'looking distraught'. 'Wearing a scarf and almost no make-up, she was scarcely recognizable as the actress who has played Meg Mortimer for seventeen years.' Harrowing pictures of the actress appeared.

The texts of some reports were more like the coverage which Crossroads had come to expect. The *Daily Mail* ran a story by their TV editor entitled 'Heartache at the Crossroads Motel', and he identified the theme of the week as far as the press was concerned: 'Soap opera took over from real life at the Crossroads Motel yesterday – though it was hard to tell the difference.' The story was written as a script for a television programme, with scenes, scripted lines, cuts, fades, and a good deal of dramatic licence. The article was correct in one thing, it certainly was difficult to tell the difference between the soap opera and real life, but whose fault was that? The press, much of which had been instrumental in attacking the programme throughout the years of its transmission, had reacted to the event by turning the people involved into characters in a drama. As the week continued there was a contrast between the reporting of the events and the construction of those events by the newspapers.

By Midsummer's Day, Wednesday 24 June, Charles Denton found himself established as the wicked controller, featured in a cartoon in *The Sun*, but for Noele Gordon and the Crossroads audience this was no dream but rather a nightmare as unfolded each day in the press. *The Sun* was supportive and ran a campaign to 'Save our Meg', and its readers voted twenty-five to one in her support. The *Star* encouraged its readers to write and suggest:

> How would YOU get rid of Meg? If Meg has to go, she has to go. But how would YOU get rid of her? Shoot her? Blow her up . . .?

The readers responded with suitably gruesome endings and the paper showed its opinion by awarding the £25 prize for the suggestion that Meg be beaten to death with a frying pan.

By mid-week, rather belatedly, another person entered centre stage. The producer, Jack Barton, visited the cast while they rehearsed, to deliver what the *Daily Mirror* called 'a twenty-minute morale-boosting lecture'. This was necessary because other members of the cast feared that a major catastrophe to remove Meg Mortimer could also remove them from the motel.

The *Daily Mirror* played a double game on Saturday 27 June when they carried stories covering two pages which talked of 'The Secret Love of the Crossroads Godmother', and an article entitled 'The Noele Gordon I Know' by Clifford Davis, the journalist who had written the exclusive the previous Monday. Both articles were basically supportive, ending with the writers' conviction that Crossroads would not be the same without the actress. At least the *Mirror* was faithful to Meg – but wait a moment, turn to page fifteen of the same edition and there Hilary Kingsley, writing 'In My View', is at least more truthful to the press image of Crossroads when she writes:

I'm glad Noele Gordon's days as Meg, the martyr of Cross-roads, are numbered.

If that sounds like another superior snipe at the soppy serial enjoyed by lonely souls who watch the test card if necessary, it isn't. Anyone who sat through the motel saga this week would have to admit it was no credit to British television.

Benny was mugged, blind and in hospital; Diane was ditched by the man she hoped would marry her and help her get back her son; fat Glenda was worrying about cocky Kevin and Meg herself was steely-eyed and humourless as ever at the helm.

Now ATV, fearing the standards-conscious IBA might close Crossroads for good, has decided to make changes – starting by sacking its star.

But if the seventeen-year-old show is to prosper, Meg mustn't go alone.

Her partner, dapper David Hunter, he of the terrorist son and gun-totting ex-wife, must go too.

So must daughter Jill. She of the broken marriage, drink, drugs and unseen babies. And we must say goodbye to Di, the much-divorced waitress.

In fact the scriptwriters should devise a general clearing scheme. It really doesn't matter what ruse they use. Perhaps Benny could be sent to a blind home and the others could help David, who is always flitting off to the Channel Islands, run a branch in Jersey.

Then the old-guard writers and directors should pack their bags.

A new-look Crossroads with life-like characters and plaus-ible stories might just become something to be proud of.

Hilary Kingsley in fact suggests that virtually the whole cast, scriptwriters, and production team be replaced, in the in-terests of the serial, of course, but perhaps without consideration of the audience. What is interesting about the attacks which are made in the popular press is that their readers constitute a large part of the Crossroads audience and the double game of outcry and attack which they played in response to the sacking of the actress can hardly be seen as reflecting the views of their readers. As the week ended there was a certain amount of anticipation and even trepidation as to the coverage and revelations which the story would receive in the 'Sundays'. The wait was not in vain. At national level, perhaps predictably, the quality papers, *The Observer*, the *Sunday Telegraph* and the mid-brow *Sunday Express* did not carry the story. However, the *Sunday Times* did carry a story about the financial difficulties of Lord Lew Grade's Associated Communications Corporation, which ended with mention of the events at Crossroads. In reaction to Lord Grade's comment that he would remain chairman and chief executive of ACC until 2001, Nick Gilbert, who wrote the article, ended with what now appears as inspired fortune-telling: 'But nothing is entirely sacrosanct in the ACC world – even Noele Gordon is to leave ATV's Crossroads.'

Amongst the Sunday 'populars', the *News of the World* had scooped 'Noele's story' in a much-heralded £60,000 deal. Their front-page story centred on the strain that the actress had undergone and since they had the exclusive contract for any comments which Noele Gordon could make to the press, they ran her opinions on the action of ATV and particularly exploited the personal aspects of the whole affair. Meanwhile, in her own story of her life, Noele Gordon set about offering the 'real Noele Gordon's story', which was understandable since for seventeen years her public personality had been intertwined with that of the character she had played. Since she was now being removed from the programme it was obviously necessary for her to re-establish her own identity as Noele Gordon.

The *Sunday Mirror* ran their front-page story with a headline half a page high. 'Noele's desperate plea, "SAVE ME, LEW!" But TV star stays axed. The real inside story by Gordon Blair.' Blair's story was itself written as a drama with the people involved cast in acting roles: Noele Gordon, the wronged actress, appealing for help to her long-time friend and head of ACC, Lord Grade. Charles Denton was again featured as the villain of the piece and Lord Grade admitted to putting the proposition to him as to whether there was any way that she could carry on. Hidden behind this little drama was Lord Grade's own drama with ATV, since the award of the franchise to ATV in the last round of awards by the IBA had included the proviso that forty-nine per cent of the shares in the new company had to be sold by ACC,

Lord Grade's company, and a new company, with a new name
and identity, be formed. Accordingly it must be recognized that
Lord Grade had little if any influence long term with ATV. Of
the actress, he said: 'She is a very sweet person and has worked
very hard for Crossroads and ATV. But I do not know whether
she has any future role in the network.' Charles Denton was
reported as saying that he had had hundreds of letters of protest
from Crossroads fans and admitted: 'I really didn't know there
were such Crossroads fanatics.' He continued to maintain that he
did not know how she would be written out of the serial. In
lighthearted, facetious style he is reported as saying, 'Concorde
could fall out of the sky and hit her on the head. She could be
hit by a bus or swallowed by a whale. We will have to wait and
see.'

Charles Denton went on to assure the viewers that the serial
would continue and Jack Barton set about the task of reassuring
the cast that the serial would continue. The reassurance was
necessary because only Miss Gordon was on an ATV staff contract and any of the other performers could be dismissed. In the
newspaper he is reported as saying:

> It has to be said no one person is bigger than the programme.
>   There are also another twelve actors on the series and they
> all have their own following too.
>   I don't want to sound hard but I'm not worried about Noele.
> She can look after herself. She is a strong person.

He also promised the viewers: 'It will be absolutely spectacular.
It will be even better than who shot JR. You will never have seen
anything like it before.' The scene was set for the next few months
of speculation as to how the character would be written out of
the series.

Since the 'scoop' story had been taken by the *News of the
World*, the other popular Sundays had to make do with lesser
beings. The *Sunday People* offered a story from John Bentley
who had played the part of Hugh Mortimer, Meg's TV husband
for eleven years but who had been written out of the serial two
years previously. His story was bitter and hostile to the actress
and he continued the theme of mixing fact with fiction throughout his story. It warrants comment only because it illustrates the

mingling of personal and professional lives as constructed through newspaper stories. His comments about their wedding confused the real and fictional aspects of their relationship.

> Our 'marriage' was the TV wedding of the year back in 1975. For her it wasn't just a performance. I'm convinced she wished it were for real . . . Whenever we played intimate scenes Nolly always melted in my arms and gave me very special loving looks – not that I ever felt anything in return.

It seems strange that he suggests that she would have wished the marriage were 'for real' since in the rest of the article he denounces her for being unfriendly towards him when not acting. Since the actress had to 'act' the romantic association with him it seems slightly unfair to criticize her for successfully portraying affection for him even if she did not actually feel it. What the story did show was that there were, of course, difficulties in appearing in a long-running series and that performers do not always see eye-to-eye or become firm friends off screen.

Some familiar themes ran through the coverage in the Sunday press – familiar, that is, to actresses. 'What about femininity, love and marriage?' asked the press. There is a need to stereotype women into categories which run, 'How do they manage to have a marriage and a career?', or 'How they sacrificed marriage for a career'. Noele Gordon has never married and the latter theme was never far from the stories. Familiar headlines ran, 'The secret man in Noele Gordon's life' (*Weekend Mirror*) and the personal life of the actress was mingled with the news stories.

One of the most sensible articles written at the time was by Clifford Davis in the *Daily Mirror*, on 27 June. He wrote:

> She isn't all that different to the lady you know as Meg Mortimer.
> They talk the same. They look the same . . . Noele has always admitted she is no great actress.
> On screen, she plays herself.

That is too simple a dismissal of acting but it does help to define the outcry which the audience felt and expressed about the sacking of the actress and the impending death of the character. The audience felt justifiable anger at the treatment of the actress and their loss of the character. They soon began to make their feelings known.

Meanwhile, back at the ATV studios, for Mike Hollingsworth, the editor of the regional news programme, ATV Today, an interesting story had broken literally along the corridor. The head of his company had sacked one of the employees and the story was clearly of news value. The actress had also agreed to be interviewed by their reporter. Mike Hollingsworth had also considered asking Charles Denton to appear on the programme, to be interviewed about his decision, and had checked with the local officer of the Independent Broadcasting Authority (IBA) whether it would be permissible for him to appear. In the event, Mike Hollingsworth decided not to arrange the interview, although it would have been permissible, and they simply ran the story, including the interview at the rehearsal rooms, with Noele Gordon. In the late afternoon the reporter on the story came to ask if Mike wanted to view the film, and both he and the head of news and current affairs at ATV went to the viewing room to see the short item. The reporter said that he had chosen film where the actress was not hostile to the television company, although she did tell the film crew at one point, 'You wouldn't be here if it weren't for me,' reminding them of her long association and work for the company.

The decision to cover the item was clearly a delicate one, and I asked Mike Hollingsworth why he had decided that it was a newsworthy story. He answered:

It really comes down to whether you think the story about television, especially in the region, is worth covering anyway. I mean, my view is that a story about something that's happened, if something has happened on television and your viewers are television viewers . . . then its an interesting event . . . Everyone knows Noele Gordon and she is well seen around this region, and drama in the television studio of the real kind, instead of the tape, is obviously something that we would cover. We did, if you remember, with The Archers, when they killed off Doris Archer. We actually covered that. The BBC didn't, strangely, and the BBC guys were absolutely delighted when we covered it. I think it's an important thing in people's lives which is centred in the region, broadcasting centred in the region.

The question of whether it was a strange experience to be reporting from their 'own house', so to speak, was something which Mike saw as irrelevant. He saw the item in purely journalistic terms in relation to his audience.

MH   We treated it as a story within the programme of real-life drama.

DH   Was that a strange situation to be in because you were talking about your own company?

MH   No, I don't actually find that strange. I think there are people within this building who do, who cannot conceive of how we can stand outside ourselves and look at ourselves, and quite often you get directions from up above saying, 'You uncover this! You uncover that!' I don't like this because you can't when it's connected with the customers, because what you do is you look at the other members of the media to see how they are covering events inside the region and you think to yourself, 'We should be just as able to cover that event as they are.' And I think it's possible to be dispassionate. It is really. I mean we're all journalists. We're all used to things that come fairly close to us and having to sit outside of them.

In fact, what the television news programme is reacting to is largely dependent on the stories which are covered in the press. The links are clearly expressed when Mike Hollingsworth talks about his programme in relation to newspapers:

MH   When you make your judgement on news you automatically have an eye to what other people are taking as their news lines, and television programmes of our sort tend to rate subjects in relation to national press. Newsnight is really the *Telegraph* or *The Guardian* style of programme. We say our programme is a cross between the *Daily Mirror* and *The Sun* appeal, or maybe the *Daily Mail*. It gives you an immediate shorthand way of giving your colleagues a sort of idea of where your levels of sensationalism and responsible journalism and popular jour-

nalism, exactly at what level you take it. I think we would
say we are *Daily Mirror/Sun* to *Daily Mail* and as a result
we look at how they react to things like Crossroads and
you only have to look at what they did.

However, the decision to send the film crew to the rehearsal
rooms had to be taken on the Monday morning before the news
story had developed during the day and when the decision was
taken only the *Daily Mirror* had run their exclusive story. But
there had been a 'hint' the day before and it was to this that they
had also reacted.

MH   The story broke on the Sunday and we had a gut reaction
      to it then. We knew it was going to be our sort of story.
      Just like any story at the moment about Princess Diana is
      our sort of story.

What he means by 'our sort of story' is stories with human interest, and above all the story about Noele Gordon was a human
interest story which both press and television journalists knew
would appeal to their audiences.

During that week in June no one at ATV quite expected the
absolute barrage of letters and telephone calls which they received
from viewers. It might be suggested that they should have known
that the viewers would react with such anger at the sacking of
the star of their most popular programme, and they did expect a
reaction, but it was the sheer magnitude of the response which
was most surprising. The hostile reaction was towards Charles
Denton, but it was administrative offices within the company
which had to deal with the onslaught. The ATV switchboard was
the first line of defence or comfort to the viewers and did try to
deal with as many calls as they could. Next came the Crossroads
office, where the women who work on the programme had to
deal with the calls and the distraught or angry viewers. However,
the departments which took the full brunt of the results of the
action were the audience relations department and the press
office. The work load in the audience relations department increased considerably because it was they who had the job of
replying to all the letters which were sent to Charles Denton or
the company. They sent out a stock letter, which thanked the

writers for their letters but basically reiterated the sentiments of the original press report.

The press office was also inundated with calls, but the people working there were not themselves fully aware of what was going on. In fact, it appears that no one knew exactly what was happening or, more importantly, why it had happened. It seems that even now Charles Denton alone is aware of why the decision was taken and he maintains that the decision was a professional one regarding the development of the serial.

One of the reasons for the confusion on Monday 22 June was that although Noele Gordon, her agent Michael Summerton and her friend and co-star in Crossroads Tony Adams had known about the sacking for two weeks before the *News of the World* speculated about the sacking on 21 June, ATV had been waiting for the actress to make the announcement and she had chosen not to reveal it until this date. Press reports of the surprise which everyone experienced upon hearing the news were not exaggerated. The director for the week was himself amazed to arrive at the rehearsal rooms on the Monday morning to find the press waiting and the actress arriving in a shocked and emotional state. The producer, Jack Barton, was not available because he always spends Mondays in London, casting for the programme. Charles Denton was away at the ITV controllers' Monday meeting, so that the various departments and staff at ATV were left to hold the fort against the onslaught of excited, story-hungry press and distraught viewers.

Press coverage of the events surrounding television programmes has always been considerable. The popular press in particular have a large area of their newspapers devoted not only to 'guides' or details of television and radio programmes but also to articles about the television personalities and their personal and professional lives. All programmes attract this coverage, but with a long-running serial which is continuous there are not the same 'pegs' on which a story can easily be hung. When a situation comedy series or a popular drama series records a new series the press can base a story on the novelty value of its 'returning to our screens'. They can remind viewers of the characters and their stories. On British television only Crossroads and Coronation Street have the continuous form, and even Emmerdale Farm and some of the newer soap operas like Take the High Road or Taff Acre have periods when they are not on the screen. Accordingly, with no novelty value, the press stories which are picked up about Crossroads and Coronation Street are often in relation to 'special events' – weddings, disasters, divorces, deaths – and these tend to be treated in mocking terms as if this is the staple, everyday content of the programmes. In fact, many weeks of episodes go by without any spectacular happenings but these weeks would not be seen as good stories for the press. It is precisely the combination of the everyday and the extraordinary which lures the press into sniping at Crossroads. If there is nothing very original to say, then a side-swipe at Crossroads seems fair game for some copy.

However, despite press and institutional attacks on Crossroads, one indisputable facet of the phenomenon remains. The programme continues to be highly attractive to and defended by its fans. Some may have felt that the amount of press coverage given to the events in Crossroads during the week of 22 June was excessive. The features editor of the *Birmingham Evening Mail*, Clem Lewis, commented on this when he wrote on 27 June that there had been some criticism about the front-page coverage which the paper had given to the story when there were so many more important issues of unemployment, violence, muggings, death and disasters. While agreeing with the sentiments expressed about the importance of other social issues, he identified the appeal of the serial for its audience:

> To them Crossroads is a warm-hearted, real-life tale. The characters at the motel are like personal friends. And Nolly Gordon, as Meg, is for them a typical, hard-working, decent, clean-living woman. Her sacking – and the decision to remove Meg from the motel – is a human story.

Perhaps the most surprising aspect of the whole affair was that there was no question but that the public would have strong opinions on the incident and that the event was newsworthy. Contracts in television are not always renewed and series on television come and go, yet the appeal of a programme like Crossroads and its sister serial Coronation Street is such that the events in and around them do evoke emotive responses from their audiences. Soap operas have become part of contemporary popular culture, and what we should be asking is, 'Why does the series warrant such support from its audience and remain so popular?'

CHAPTER 2

What is Soap Opera?

Soap operas began in the 1930s in America as radio serials which were sponsored by the giant soap powder manufacturers like Proctor and Gamble. They wanted to create programmes which would attract women listeners and sell their products – soap powder. 'Soaps' have always been seen as escapist or fantasy programmes through which women could realize the romance missing from their own everyday lives. Nicknamed by their critics 'washboard weepies', they were instantly successful and instantly derided. Their success puzzled and amazed their critics, some of whom dismissed them as trivia for women, while others sought more seriously to define what it was about them that appealed to their audience. There has always been a tendency to worry about their 'effect' on their listeners. They remained great audience pullers and the form transferred naturally to television as that service expanded. America has always had many soap operas and they have become less derided as time has progressed. Indeed many of the serials shown on BBC television are imports of expensively-produced, high-gloss American television soap operas.

Critical attention to American soap operas has come from academic studies and more popular journals as well as newspapers. Indeed there is a magazine industry linked to the programmes and *Soap Opera Digest* keeps readers up to date with the storylines of the soap operas on their screens. In July 1974, in an article in the *New York Times* by Peter Funt entitled 'Game Shows Now Dominate Daytime TV', he suggested that for reasons of economy game shows were now the dominant form on daytime television and reported one network vice-president as saying the soap operas had run their course. In fact, currently soap operas in America are enjoying immense popularity and within the last three years the daytime serials and their stars have become, in some cases, more popular than many night-time television shows. Famous and established film stars appear in major roles in the shows and also make weekly guest appearances.

One major difference between the genre as it has developed in America and Britain is the vast budgets which are allocated to soap operas in the USA. But even with the large outlay on their production, they attract such lucrative advertising revenue that they are still immensely profitable to their owners who are usually the advertising agencies or the sponsors, unlike the British programmes which are the property of the television company which produces them. Despite the different financial bases there are many elements from American soap operas which have been taken up by the British versions.

It would be impossible for me to discuss American soap operas fully in this book, but the following extract from an article by Tania Modleski, 'The Search for Tomorrow in Today's Soap Operas', which appeared in *Film Quarterley*, Fall 1979, gives enough information about the formula for American soap operas to see where they link with and differ from the soap operas which we see in Britain:

The Soap Formula
Currently twelve soap operas are shown daily, each half an hour or an hour long. The first goes on the air at about 10 am, and they run almost continuously until approximately 3.30 pm. With the exception of Ryan's Hope, which takes place in a big city, the soaps are set in small towns and involve two or three families intimately connected with one another. Families are often composed of several generations and the proliferation of generations is accelerated by the propensity of soap characters to mature at an incredibly rapid rate. Thus the matriarch on Days of Our Lives, who looks to be about sixty-five, has managed over the years to become a great-great-grandmother. Occasionally one of the families will be fairly well to do, and another will be somewhat lower on the social scale though still, as a rule, identifiably middle-class. In any case, since there is so much intermingling and intermarrying, class distinctions quickly become hopelessly blurred. Children figure largely in many of the plots, but they don't appear on the screen all that often, nor do the very old. Blacks and other minorities are almost completely excluded.

Women as well as men frequently work outside the home,

usually in professions such as law and medicine, and women are generally on a professional par with men. But most of everyone's time is spent experiencing and discussing personal and domestic crises. Kathryn Weibel* lists some of the most frequent themes:

the evil woman
the great sacrifice
the winning back of an estranged lover/spouse
marrying her for her money, respectability, etc
the unwed mother
deceptions about the paternity of children
career vs housewife
the alcoholic woman (and occasionally man).

Controversial social problems are introduced from time to time. Rape was recently an issue on several soap operas and was, for the most part, handled in a sensitive manner. In spite of the fact that soaps contain more references to social problems than do most other forms of mass entertainment, critics tend to fault them heavily for their lack of social realism. As for the fans, most insist on soap opera's extreme lifelikeness and claim that the characters have to cope with problems very like their own.

The link between the American soap operas and the current British television programmes is through the radio serials. BBC radio has sustained long-running daily serials, as well as shorter family serials. Their first long-running serial was The Dales, which began as Mrs Dale's Diary, and ran from 5 January, 1948 until the 25 April, 1969. The programme was transmitted in the afternoon and repeated the next morning for those who had missed it or wanted to listen again. It concentrated on the everyday lives of the heroine's family, relayed through the story which she told. Her most famous phrase, 'I'm worried about Jim', epitomized the role of the mother figure, who dominates the soap-opera form, and it established a link between Mrs Dale and all her female listeners. Mrs Dale was wife, mother, mother-in-law,

* Kathryn Weibel, *Mirror, Mirror, Images of Women Reflected in Popular Culture* (New York, Anchor Books, 1977).

grandmother, friend, neighbour, employer, and she juggled her life playing every role. She was unashamedly middle class, but her role as doctor's wife enabled her to cut across class – at least, within the programme. The confidentialities of her news, gossip and worries about the problems of her family and friends were entrusted to her diary but listeners were allowed to eavesdrop as Mrs Dale's thoughts were transferred to the pages of the airwaves.

As The Dales finished on Friday 25 April, 1969 the BBC did not leave their listeners without a daily radio serial and Waggoner's Walk replaced it on Monday 28. This concentrated on the lives of a series of families and people not living in family situations, and was located in a fictional street. This series fell victim to BBC economy cuts in 1980 and only The Archers has now survived as a long-running daily radio soap opera.

The Archers had an introductory trial week from 29 May to 2 June, 1950, then an introductory programme on 28 December, 1950, and began daily transmission from 1 January, 1951. It has continued every night with an omnibus edition on Sunday mornings. The Archers works on the basis of a family story, but one which is much more located in the fictional village of Ambridge, and the sense of locality and farming within the country community has always been a strong theme within the programme. Also there was a conscious inclusion of information concerned with the farming community, indeed it was a feature of its original creation.

The 1960s was the time when soap operas emerged as a new type of programme on television. Although the BBC had transmitted 146 weekly episodes of The Groves between 9 April, 1954 and 28 June, 1957, it was the advent of Granada's Coronation Street, first transmitted on 9 December, 1960, which seems to have encouraged a flurry of soap operas both on BBC television and with ITV companies. The BBC produced Compact – the story of life on a women's magazine – written by Peter Ling and Hazel Adair, who were later to move to start Crossroads. Compact had 373 twice-weekly episodes and ran from January, 1962 to July, 1965. In October 1965 the BBC began two new serials which ran on alternate nights of the week. United began on 4 October and ran until March 1967. This serial told the story of the fortunes of a football club. On 5 October, 1965 The Newcomers, the BBC's longest-running serial, began and continued until 13

November, 1969, with 430 episodes transmitted. This told the story of a family moving to a new town. The themes of these early soap operas were always rooted in the contemporary social scene. During this period Coronation Street became nationally successful and ATV's Emergency Ward 10, as well as the relatively new Crossroads, were running and it was obviously a time when the BBC was committed to the soap-opera form. Since then, however, they have not had any continuous soap operas although they have been committed to the ideas within the genre, but have preferred the series form which has a predetermined number of episodes. In recent years they have had The Brothers, Angels, and Triangle, all of which concentrated on the problems and interests of the characters' personal lives. Apart from The Brothers, however, which did have a central matriarchal figure, the other programmes have had a range of characters but without the 'mother figure' of soap operas. Angels had concentrated particularly on the inclusion of social and moral issues and intertwined them with the lives of the characters with great success.

In 1978 the BBC transmitted the first episode of Dallas at 8.10 pm on a Tuesday evening. It very quickly became a success and was moved to the prime Saturday evening slot where twenty-four million viewers watched to see the much-publicized shooting of JR. The American producers of Dallas held the audience in suspense with a cliffhanger of 'Who Shot JR?' over many months while a new series was made. Dallas is a glossy, glamorous version of the American soap operas, and its success on British television was followed by the BBC's purchase of Knot's Landing and Flamingo Road. These have high-cost budgets and high-standard production values and present an image to British viewers which is far from their own everyday life experiences. Yet they contain the vital ingredient for success in relation to the audience for soap operas – personal problems and emotional entanglements. They do provide escapism to exotic locations, but even so, they are firmly rooted in the everyday problems of extremely rich and privileged people.

Commercial television has always needed to catch an audience and began at a disadvantage, since the BBC was already installed with loyal viewers when the new independent companies began in 1955. Soap operas had always attracted large audiences in America and they were a natural genre to be part of the programmes in Britain. Coronation Street and Crossroads have been the longest-running serials on British television, but ATV's Emergency Ward 10 was also very popular in the early 60s. Independent television has always had a commitment to the soap-opera form and has produced many well remembered and popular series over the years. ATV in particular has produced The Cedar Tree and For Maddie with Love, and more recently Southern began Together in 1980. Many of the programmes produced by the independent companies have been produced to fill the lunch-time drama schedule, which is at 1.30 after the News at One programme. Emmerdale Farm, from Yorkshire, began in that slot in 1972 and progressed to an evening slot when it proved to be successful. It is now one of the three continuous serials running on ITV channels.

Currently, there are two soap operas running in the lunchtime slot: Taff Acre, which was produced by HTV and set in Wales, began its first series in 1981, and STV's Take the High Road, set in the fictional village of Glendarroch in Scotland, whose first series was transmitted in February 1980. Both deal with communities which are rooted in the locality and reflect the culture and countryside of their region. This is a definite production aim to satisfy the IBA's regulation that the independent companies which hold the franchise for a particular region should make programmes which reflect that region. The listing of programmes which are made in the soap-opera form but which have a limited production run highlights an aspect of the development of the long-running, continuous soap operas. For in effect the production company does not set out to make a soap opera to run for five, ten or twenty years. They start off by making a predetermined number of episodes and it is purely the viewers' reception of the programmes which determines whether they develop into a show that runs indefinitely. In this sense, when Granada and ATV began Coronation Street and Crossroads in the 1960s they did not know that they were beginning serials which would become so popular.

Coronation Street is Britain's longest-running television serial, celebrating its twenty-first birthday in December 1981. It is transmitted twice weekly, on Monday and Wednesday evenings at 7.30 pm. It is also a feature of British contemporary culture, firmly located in the north of England and seen as reflecting the values of that region. Like Crossroads, it has always been tremendously popular, rarely out of the ratings, but it has not been subject to the same hostile criticism. However, some critics do lump the two programmes together to dismiss them collectively. Coronation Street claims to reflect 'working-class culture', and it is strongly rooted in the traditional cultural working-class values of the 1950s period. In some respects the series is still located in the period of the early 60s when it began. It is realistic, but its realism is often slightly solidified in the earlier period. This does not detract from its strength in production values, scripts and acting. In fact it is a feature of the programme. However, it must be said that if Coronation Street were reflecting the reality of the north in the 1970s and 80s there might be at least one black family living on the street. One of the main strengths of the serial is its glittering array of women characters, incorporating their values and humour, and providing some of the few women on television to whom the audience can relate.

There is a tradition of comparing Crossroads and Coronation Street but I do not intend to participate in that tendency. The comparisons can lead to a divisive attitude towards the genre. Both programmes have their own strengths and values, both in production and in intention. They share some qualities and each possesses qualities of its own. Coronation Street, for instance, has never been as committed to the inclusion of topics of social concern as Crossroads, but its handling of areas of concern in the everyday life of its women characters incorporates a deep commitment to women's cultural values. It has taken the best traditional elements of the drama of soap opera and used them to develop a style which is unmistakeably its own.*

There are basic differences between a serial and a series. A serial has established characters and settings and an unfolding narrative whose plots or storylines continue over from one episode to another. A series consists of self-contained episodes although it has the same characters and situations. Often the story is complete within each episode. There is also the form of the serialized series which, although having some characteristics of a serial, has

* For a fuller analysis of Coronation Street, see the BFI Monograph no 13, *Coronation Street*, by Richard Dyer, *et al.*

a pre-decided number of episodes. This is the form of many of
the series which the BBC produce. Broadly speaking, soap operas
like Crossroads and Coronation Street are serials; series are the
usual form of situation comedy programmes like The Good Life,
Butterflies, Porridge, etc; and the serialized series are the form
of the BBC programmes such as Angels, The Brothers, Triangle.

Soap operas create the illusion that the characters and the
location exist and continue whether the viewers are there or not.
They invite their viewers to drop in and see the characters and
share their lives, but the illusion depends on the credibility that
life goes on, even when the viewers are not watching. A very
basic definition of soap opera is that it is a continuous drama
serial which should be transmitted daily. In this sense there are
no soap operas on British television, but 'Crossroads' was transmitted daily when it began.

Soap opera has a specific location and a core set of characters
around whose lives the main storylines are woven. There are additional characters who may come and go and whose lives in some
way touch those of the main characters. Each episode has a number
of themes or stories running through it and there is a cliff-
hanger at the end of the episode to hold the audience in suspense
until the next episode, and to encourage them to watch again.

These serials have traditionally offered a range of strong
female characters and this has proved a popular feature of the
genre for its audience. They show women of different ages, class
and personality types, and offer characters with whom many
members of their female audience can empathize. They also
include male characters often for romantic interest, sometimes as
comic characters or 'bad' characters, but in the main the men do
not have the leading roles within the serials. There are few
children in soap operas, which does tend to detract from their
representation of 'real life', but this is caused by the difficulties
in sustaining babies and children in a long-running serial.

Some soap operas do have definite aims to include areas of
social concern which are interwoven with the lives of the characters within the drama. They are designed specifically to connect
with everyday life and aim to reflect reality. Soap operas are
about people and the problems of their everyday lives. The location may be a family, a farming community, a northern street or

a hospital ward, a motel or the ranch of a Texas oil millionaire; and the drama may show a work situation in a hospital ward, or people at leisure in the corner pub; but this is always secondary to the main theme of the drama. [Primarily soap operas are about the problems of everyday personal life and personal relationships. They may include representations of class, work or gender, but they cut across classes by sharing with their predominantly female audience the problems which are experienced by women whatever their age or class.]

Soap operas take the form of the continuous serial whose internal time is supposed to coincide with 'real' time. However, time in the serial is restricted to calendar time, the day or week, not to time of day. The coincidence with real time is not normally emphasized in the programmes but it is highlighted when special calendar times, like Christmas and New Year or Valentine's Day, are made part of the events within the serial, with appropriate reference being made both visually and in the storylines. The programme-makers are on pretty sure ground that Christmas will occur as scheduled each year to coincide with the events within their programme. However, they also tend to reference 'important' events which are happening in the 'real world', if they are of such significance as to detract from the reality of the programme if they are not mentioned. This involves more of a risk for them because, although scheduled, there is always the possibility that something could happen to prevent the event happening and then a reference within the programme would be disastrous in terms of destroying the illusion and could possibly be embarrassing.

The decision to include reference to the Royal Wedding in July 1981 was clearly necessary in terms of the reality of the events in the Crossroads serial. The programme included a storyline which involved the staff wishing to watch the wedding while they were at work and also a toast being drunk to the royal couple by the characters in the serial. Since the programme was recorded three weeks earlier, had there been any unforeseen cancellation or hitch during the day, then the programme-makers would have had an interesting problem to deal with. They do, however, take a chance and include such references whenever possible, to add to the reality of the series.

Each scene in serials does have a time attached to it and in the case of Crossroads the scene may be headed 'The Brownlows', 6.30 pm', or 'The motel kitchen, 6.35'. As a feature for the viewer this is not noticeable, but it is used by the production team in their creation of the sense of time within the programme.

Because time is continuous and seemingly infinite in a soap opera it does mean that there is no need for any storyline to have a final resolution. Indeed it is only through the death or removal of one of the characters or the ending of the serial that anything 'final' happens in soap operas. To try to introduce an 'ending' in this sense is an event which, as we have seen, brings down the wrath of the viewers on the programme-makers.

Two familiar but contradictory statements are often heard about soap operas. Apparently 'nothing happens' in them, they just crawl along from one banal situation to another. Conversely, they are said to thrive on continual crises, leaping from one terrible scene of domestic trivia to another. Actually these positions are not so very far apart. What links them is what they tell us about the perspective of the critic. It is correct to define 'the domestic' and 'the personal' as the main domains of soap opera, but to see the events within them as banal and over-dramatized is to ignore their main strengths. Soap operas, along with situation comedies, are not seen either by their creators or their viewers as a vehicle for progressive or revolutionary ideas, but they do present a liberal view of the consensus. Programme-makers in these areas see that the area of progressivism is one which belongs to the single play or the documentary, but they do feel that they can get messages of social concern across to their audience where other programmes may fail. Soap opera tends to stay within the idea of 'balanced programmes' in the same way that news and current affairs programmes do, and they offer alternate views of events or situations and air a problem from different perspectives or points of view. However, the continuous narrative means that although certain storylines may be resolved for the moment, there is always the possibility that mistakes can be rectified later and there is a potential for growth and change within the serial form. Also, the actual raising of problems which are seen as relevant to their lives is a progressive form in terms of women viewers. There are very few other programmes to which they respond and which they enjoy in the same way as soap operas.

CHAPTER 3

The Journey to the Crossroads Motel

I don't make programmes for critics – I make programmes for the viewers.

Lord Grade

Crossroads would seem to be the most maligned programme on British television. Alone among the few soap operas currently appearing on our screens, it is at the same time enormously popular and yet devastatingly criticized. The removal of its leading character, Meg Mortimer, was seen by some as a potential death blow to a drama series whose own story has been as dramatic as some of the storylines within it. There can be few people who could honestly admit never to have heard of Crossroads and it has, like it or not, become a part of contemporary popular culture.

Crossroads was first transmitted on British television at 6.30 pm on 2 November, 1964 in the ATV region. By January 1965 it was taken by some of the network companies, others soon followed and since then it has been shown right across the country. There was a time when Thames did drop it from its schedules, but pressure from the public forced the company to reinstate the programme. It has rarely been out of the ratings and has attracted an audience averaging fourteen or fifteen million over the seventeen years of the transmission. It all began with a request sent to various writers:

What is needed is a soap opera, five days a week across the board, to go out at 4.30 for twenty-five minutes. A programme that would appeal in the main to the housewife – a kind of Mrs Dale's Diary – but one that would reflect the Midland life and could at the same time be acceptable in the rest of the country. Not as broad as Coronation Street, realizing that it is in the afternoon. The sets could not be large, nor moved about too much. The cast would be small and, of course, new characters could be introduced now and again and we could use a number of extras . . .

Sir Lew Grade

From the responses which he received to his original request, Lord Grade approached Hazel Adair and Peter Ling, who were then working on the BBC series Compact, and asked them to devise a series based on the idea of a story about two sisters, which was to be called Midland Road. The writers were not happy to work with someone else's original idea and developed their own version. The title was changed to Crossroads, which was to be both the name of the motel and signify the Midlands as the crossroads of the country, and also the 'crossroads of the lives of the two sisters in the serial'.

The original concept had included the soap-opera convention of rivalry between two sisters, Meg representing the 'good', and Kitty the 'bad'. Peter Ling recalls that it was the viewers' reaction to the story of Meg and her more glamorous life compared with that of her sister which led to that part of the story being developed as the main topic of the serial. Meg had decided to turn her Georgian home into a motel after her husband's death, and her sister Kitty Jarvis was living in a more seedy area of the back streets of industrial Birmingham. The clash and rivalry between the two sisters was intended to be the pivot for the story, but the combination of the viewers' reaction, commented on by Peter Ling, and the actresses' portrayal of the characters, which according to Noele Gordon 'turned out much nicer than anyone expected', meant that the stories developed in a different way. Whatever the reason for the change in the convention that sisters are always rivals and jealous of each other, Crossroads made a positive development in terms of not showing sisters in hostility with one another, but as friends. The love and sharing of troubles between sisters is now, of course, the subject of the American programme Soap.

The Crossroads story is about the life of Meg Mortimer and her two children, Sandy and Jill. The motel is situated in the fictional village of Kings Oak, which is located on the road between Birmingham and Stratford-upon-Avon at the crossroads of a road which geographically would lead to Coventry in the east and Redditch in the west. Round about are fictional villages of Heathbury in the direction of Birmingham and Merryfields to the south in the direction of Stratford. Although all the locations are fictional, Birmingham appears in the serial as the city to which the characters travel for important shopping and business. The original story also concerned Meg's sister Kitty and her husband, and they had a brother, Andy. The stories revolved round them and their families and the characters in the village who worked at the motel.

The idea of a motel was the ideal location for a soap opera because the management and staff provide the basic core of characters, and the transitory nature of guests visiting the motel gives the possibility for additional characters to be in the series for a short time. In the early days there was much more emphasis on 'stars' or personalities making guest appearances as visitors who 'dropped in' at the motel to see Meg, and this added to the blurred edges between fiction and show-business reality. This is no longer a feature of the series as the present producer believes that it detracts from the viewers' belief in the reality of the motel.

The programme has been criticized for not reflecting the Midlands area, but if that is determined by the arbitrary cutting up of the country into a region for the holding of television franchise, it is not surprising. It certainly may not reflect Nottingham, nor Oxfordshire, nor Gloucestershire, but those areas all have their own identity. It is, however, unmistakeably rooted in the West Midlands, Birmingham and the surrounding area. Over the years some of the characters have been definitely based on the Birmingham region, and the excellent portrayal of the 'Brummie' Jim Baines, by the actor John Forgeham could be held as an effective reflection of a Birmingham character. Of course, there are many people living in the West Midlands. However, it should be remembered that the concept of a motel works on the principle that there are visitors and these are not likely to have Midlands accents, which is one of the criteria by which the programme appears to have been judged for its authenticity. The size of the work force of the West Midlands, until the recent economic devastation, has meant that there have always been a large variety of people coming there from other parts of the country and the world. Crossroads has been anxious to reflect the cultural and ethnic groups in the area and has had a number of black and Asian families and characters in the storylines. Currently it has the character of Mac, the black garage mechanic who is working at the motel garage and becoming increasingly more important in storylines.

Inevitably a programme which has had people associated with it for a long period becomes also the story of those personalities. Crossroads has always been the story of Meg Richardson and Noele Gordon. Noele Gordon was already established in the ATV region as a presenter both of a tea-time chat-show, Tea with Noele Gordon, which began in 1957, and Lunch Box, which was a combination of a chat-show with light entertainment. Lunch Box finished after eight years, as she transferred to the leading role in Crossroads. She became instantly successful in the role and made the transition from presenting, projecting her own personality, to the role of acting the fictional character. Yet to many viewers the personality and the character have always been intertwined – not confused, but very much merged together. The initial and continuing popularity of the serial has been largely associated with the success and popularity of the actress and her sustaining of the character for seventeen years.

When the series began, its producer, Reg Watson, had no experience of producing a daily soap opera, nor for that matter had anyone else in Britain, but it was his efforts in the years that he produced the programme that established it as a popular success. Indeed, he had been instrumental in discussing American soap opera with Lew Grade a few years before the programme began. The producer's role in the production of a programme does, of course, determine the style which the programme reflects. Reg Watson's personality greatly influenced the programme for the ten years that he produced it and the development of the first ten years of Crossroads is related in Noele Gordon's book, *My Life at Crossroads.**

Margaret French, who has been the production manager on the programme since it began, told me some details of the beginnings of Crossroads. She has always been responsible, with the producer, for casting the programme, as well as for the day-to-day production control, and is a vital person in the production. The development in the early days was clearly rooted in the soap-opera tradition, but linked with repertory theatre:

*Noele Gordon, *My Life at Crossroads* (Star Books, 1975).

MF   My main involvement with Reg really was finding the cast,
     which was quite a marathon, and we went to the Birmingham
     Rep and the Alex Theatre, who at that time had their
     own rep company. We virtually stole everyone in the Alex
     Theatre's rep. company. They were suddenly told that
     they were going to be given a twelve-month contract, at
     what then seemed an enormous amount of money, which
     took all their breath away. Plus the fact of twelve months
     security of work. However, the auditions that they had to
     go through were coming for an interview in the morning
     and reading a script, going away at lunchtime with the
     script, coming back in the afternoon having had to learn
     it, and stand in front of a camera and perform it, which
     was a very big ordeal.

DH   And really television was quite new then in terms of ex-
     perience.

MF   Well we'd been going about ten years but the actors
     hadn't had that experience, certainly not. It was probably
     the first time they'd been inside a studio.

She continued the story of how Roger Tonge had auditioned
for the part of Sandy Richardson. The extract indicates how,
from its inception, the production schedule had an effect on the
choice of performers.

MF   He'd got to come in and tell his mother that he'd just
     seen his dog run over on the motorway, the motel being
     on the motorway, and it was the final audition. The one
     boy from Sutton Coldfield, who had been to drama
     school, he came and he cried, and he cried very well, but
     he didn't say very much. And Roger came in and never
     stopped talking, and that's what got him the part, because
     the fear at that time was of that speed at which they'd
     got to learn, remembering that it was five shows a week,
     and they worked six days a week. The limitation on time
     for learning was such that you had to make sure that they
     could ad lib, that if they did dry up, they didn't stop
     talking, because we didn't have the editing facilities.
     There was no editing then at all, so it was literally as it
     happened, and it was in the very early stages of recording

because up to a very short time before then everything had to be live.

In the following extract she indicated how the programme also referenced the 'real world' and reflected contemporary ideas. The 60s was the time when motorways were being built in Britain and the concept of the motel was new.

DH So initially what was the idea that the serial was going to be about?

MF Well, it was about Meg Richardson, the widow who'd suddenly found herself in a big house which she couldn't afford to run, didn't want to leave it and they built a motorway through the land, and so she decided to capitalize on it, because at that time motels were very new in this country, and the producer, being an Australian, was very conscious of motels. I think there were about three in England at that time, because the one we used initially to establish the exteriors was in fact in Nuneaton.

The motel and its characters were established and successful in terms of their audience but for Crossroads there has always been another side to their story. Maggie French recalled, 'The newspapers slated us right from the inception. What they didn't bargain for was the public reaction.'

Even before it was transmitted there were groans of complaint that there was to be yet another soap opera on television. However, once it *was* transmitted, the dual story of Crossroads began with a vengeance, and the pattern was set which was to follow the programme throughout its career – success with the viewers and attacks from the critics. Two years after its start, ATV's director of programmes, Bill Ward, was worried by the critical attacks which were made on the programme and wanted to take it off. Lord Grade refused and supported the programme and continued to support it throughout his time at ATV. The critics also alerted the attention of the Independent Television Authority (now the IBA), who were pledged to see that the standards were maintained. The most visible official criticism has continued to come from the IBA, but it has also been attacked from within the television industry, by critics in newspapers and by a substantial section of the television audience, most markedly by those who profess never to have watched it – or maybe just once or twice. There are also many critics who profess never to watch the programme yet know all the characters and storylines.

The IBA's most recent attack on the programme came in July 1979 and this was reported in the more serious newspapers as well as the popular press. The *Daily Telegraph* reported that the IBA had told ATV that the viewing figures were not sufficient reason not to improve the quality of Crossroads. David Glencross, Deputy Director of Television at the IBA, is reported as saying:

> Despite its ratings success any programme must also rely on where it is placed in the evening schedule. At the time Crossroads is screened BBC has not started putting out its strongest programmes and BBC2 is still showing Open University.

Charles Denton was swift in defending the programme:

> We are deeply disappointed by the Authority's edict and like fifteen million viewers we do not share the IBA's opinion of Crossroads. But the Authority has absolute power to tell any ITV company what to do.

The criticism which the IBA made of Crossroads was the most public criticism ever made about a television programme. They criticized nearly every facet of the show, saying that the acting, scripts and production had fallen below required standards. Yet one year later, when Crossroads was taken off for the duration of the 1980 Olympic Games, an official of the IBA told me that they received more letters of protest from the viewers than they had about any other action.

Throughout its life, the viewers have remained loyal to the programme and registered their support in force. The programme won *The Sun* award as 'Top ITV Series' for three consecutive years from 1973 to 1975. Noele Gordon won the *TV Times* award for the 'Most Compulsive Female Character' and 'Favourite Female Personality' on eight consecutive occasions and is the first award winner to be elevated to the '*TV Times* Hall of Fame'.

*

It would be impossible to trace the history of the programme over seventeen years as one part of one chapter in a book, and I can only indicate the flavour of the programme and its reception when it first started as an insight into the current situation which encompasses Crossroads. The programme is an excellent example of the forces which are in play in relation to all programmes, but they are not normally as visible as they have been in the case of Crossroads for throughout its existence it has shown the articulation between the broadcasting institutions, the production company, the programme-makers and the audience. Jack Barton, the current producer, expresses an honest reaction to the critics and his feelings about Crossroads which sums up what the programme is about in the eyes of the programme-makers. It is perhaps revealing to juxtapose a comment, taken at random from the ATV press office newspaper cuttings on the programme, with the comment by the producer, to highlight the kind of criticism which has been levelled at the programme:

They are doing their damnedest to revive this decomposing corpse. They have used every gimmick in the book, no matter how stupid. One has only to listen to the disparaging references on TV by other artists to realize this theatrical joke has gone on long enough. An earthquake or an invasion from outer space would put the show out of its misery.

Evening News, 14.2.80

JB No, it's a programme for the viewers, not for the critics, anyway. And that's not an easy way out, it's because the critics are destructive. I'm always interested to read criticism, and if there's something constructive I can take from it, I will, obviously. But you have to accept that with a long-running serial, it is asking too much of anybody not to have bad patches. God almighty, we're not miracle workers. Everything can be criticized, you can criticize some of the most prestigious productions, but I think soap opera is an easy target, and with our relentless turn-arounds, you're going to have your highs and lows, and your good bits and bad bits.

Equally, the programme has to provide a platform for people to make mistakes. People have got to learn their trade. Every week on the floor, you'll find things are slowed down a bit because we're not getting the shots on one camera – why? – because you've got a trainee on that camera, and he's been thrown in and made to do it, jump to it. You do this programme and, by God, you've broken the back and you'll do anything. You've got technicians who've had to learn their trade on it, you have writers – we're constantly trying new writers – I will get new actors who are new to TV. Some click, some don't. Some are a disaster, but that's all part and parcel. There aren't the theatres today where people can go and learn their trade, and so soap operas are a marvellous platform for people to learn.

I asked Jack Barton what was his job as producer.

JB   The overriding responsibility I have is to adhere to my brief, which is to keep this programme high in the ratings and keep it within its budget. If it falls out of the ratings my head's on the block and a lot of people are out of work. That involves giving the viewers what they want, monitoring their reactions, which come from a variety of sources, having my finger on the pulse all the time. That doesn't mean to say I can please everybody – you can't please all of the people all of the time – but from the general consensus of the rapport that I have with the viewers, I give them what they want, and that keeps us high in the ratings. Otherwise you'd see a tremendous change, we'd begin to fall.

A television programme is a complicated combination of many different skills, ideas, practicalities, and not least, the product of many different people working together. A programme is produced, constructed, made and the end result is determined by the joint efforts of all those who are involved in the production. In respect of these considerations it must be said that Crossroads is produced and survives in spite of many and because of a few. There are some people who are completely committed to the programme, but there are others for whom working on it is a job which they do not particularly enjoy. The co-ordination of the whole production is the work of the producer and Jack Barton took over that role after Reg Watson left to return to Australia in 1975. Formerly a director on the programme and originating in the circus world and coming into television through variety, Jack Barton's attitude to television is rooted in entertainment and the audience. His role is virtually autonomous in relation to Crossroads and his commitment to the programme is total. It is interesting to consider his own background in relation to his beliefs and aims in the programme:

JB　You see, I didn't get that kind of education that you have to have today. You see, if I was starting today, I wouldn't get in, because I would not have the qualifications. The school of life is the thing that matters. They wouldn't look at you – elementary school education and at fourteen you left and ran away with the bloody circus, what kind of education is that? But my God, you learned about people, you learned about surviving. When I ran away from home and went off with the circus, I had two years with them and lived as a member of the Coco family. I learned from him, and then I went off and went on an oil tanker and went round the world. Experiences like that. And then finally I came back and got down to the business of getting into the business properly, and learning, and going to dance school, music school, and learning to play instruments, to sing, etc. And then through the hard years of the few little third-rate reviews, and gradually working your way up to big West End productions. That kind of experience all the time, meeting people, because it was all before TV, it was all touring the country, you see. In fact, meeting people in little towns and little theatres, it's all great experience that goes up there into your head, and you use it throughout your life, and exploit it and capitalize on it, because you know them. That's what you mean when you say you've got your finger on the pulse, because you know what the man in the cloth cap feels.

Paternalistic concern is a feature of Jack Barton's attitude to the content of the programme, the cast and his audience. Not that the attitude is benevolent, but rather one of professional concern to entertain and inform about certain aspects of everyday

life. He closely adheres to the policy that the audience should
'make the running' in terms of what the programme should contain. They should have a certain amount of control in determining
what goes on in the scripts. When he talks about his view of his
audience it reveals the idea of a 'national family' and cross-section
of society which he feels is reflected in the philosophy of the
programme. In an extract above he talks about the rapport which
he has with his audience. He continued:

DH   And where do you think that rapport comes from that
      you've got?

JB   It comes from, quite apart from mail, from viewers' mail,
      it comes from my own and the whole production team's
      personal involvement in their everyday lives. They live in
      various parts of the country, and they all meet their local
      friends and viewers approach *them*, when they recognize
      them, and tell them what they think about it, etc. And all
      this is feedback and it all ties in usually with the kind of
      reaction I'm getting on a personal level and the mail that
      I get.

DH   Have you actually got an image of your audience, do you
      see it as lots of different . . .? I mean who do you think
      your audience is?

JB   My audience, without question, is the widest possible
      cross-section of society. It's the mass and that covers
      everybody, and that is why you'll find in the programme
      representatives of that cross-section, so that if they can't
      identify with one group, they'll identify with another.
      And that goes from − if you want to compartmentalize
      people − from what you might call the manual workers
      up to the professional classes, and all those kind of people,
      from all walks of life, all watch. There's this identity
      thing that you have, but more important, it's like they
      feel this rendezvous, it's like feeling part of the national
      community, that we all come together, it's a bringing to-
      gether of a whole nation, and there's some security that
      comes from that kind of feeling, a unifying aspect, from
      all walks of life. That's why, when you lose a character, a
      popular character, it's why they're terribly concerned

about it, it's because it's part of their escapism and relaxation, and someone they've identified with for years.

To entertain and inform, without alienating his audience, and
to keep them hooked to his programme is vital if Jack Barton is
to achieve the other aim which he sees as being of great importance. This is the conscious inclusion of areas and topics of social
concern. In this respect Crossroads under Jack Barton has made
a definite commitment to using the soap-opera form for bringing
to the notice of the audience the problems of the disabled, the
need for kidney donors, and many more issues of social concern.
It illustrates the problems and gives the information by making
it of direct concern to characters within the series, and making it
part of the story-telling.

JB   With some of the more serious social comments that we've
      made and issues that we've dealt with, in each case they
      were very carefully thought about and researched, and
      they have had positive results to the community. The
      'Crossroads Care Attendance Scheme' is something posi-
      tive that came out of it. The contributions we made to
      kidney sufferers – we've now got a four-bedded unit for
      kids – that never existed. Those are positive things, so this
      is what makes it all so satisfying. (. . .)* But you see, an-
      other thing is, when you think of the power of soap opera
      and how people – why they listen to the social comment
      we make, it's because we obviously graft that social com-
      ment on to some of our characters and they care about
      those characters. That's why they're concerned, and that's
      how you're getting the message through. (. . .) That's the
      power of soap opera, that'll get your messages over, and a
      lot of people are frightened of it. People used to say to
      me, 'It's a lot of power, you know. Doesn't that frighten
      you?' And I'd say, 'It doesn't. I'm aware of it and there-
      fore I mustn't misuse it, I must be very careful, but cer-
      tainly I am aware.'

The power of soap opera is immense and it is not normally
recognized by the broadcasting industry as a whole. Many of the

*Denotes edit.

most socially-aware and committed people in television are working in the area of documentary programme making and are often
attempting to get over the exact messages which Jack Barton
achieves so successfully in Crossroads. The clue to the success is
certainly in the comment which he makes that the issues are
grafted on to some of their characters, and the fact that the
viewers 'care about those characters'. It is potentially a very
powerful form and the implications for its misuse could be considerable, but the possibilities for its use are equally considerable. The success of the form is also rooted in its connection with
the lives of its audience and the style of presentation of the programme. One of the criticisms which is levelled at the programme
is its simplicity, but there is a great strength in communicating a
message in an accessible way, without trivializing the message or
patronizing the viewer. The art of communication is getting your
ideas across to other people and there is little value in having
good ideas if you cannot communicate them successfully. As with
light entertainment and situation comedy, soap operas are not an
area of programming which is at the forefront of progressiveness.
Both broadcasters and audience think that pushing back the
boundaries or arousing political awareness is the business of the
single play, or a current affairs or documentary programme.
However there are areas of social concern and welfare which are
a recognized part of soap opera, and Crossroads in particular has
intertwined social comment with its fictional form.

In its position in the schedule either adjacent to or hammocking
the news and local news programmes, Crossroads is part of the
same time slot which often contains coverage of disasters, hor-
rors, murder, scenes of death (although these are to a certain
extent censored for the evening news bulletin). Yet the fictional
form of Crossroads is restricted in what it can contain because of
the IBA protective legislation in respect of the family viewing
time, which continues until 7.30 pm. This means that even if
they introduce topics which are socially contentious, like abortion
or marital sexual difficulties or whatever, they are restricted in
the way they can handle the problems.

The transmission time for Crossroads varies across the ITV
regions. Although the programme is taken by all the ITV companies, it is shown on different days and at different times,

ranging from 5.15 to 6.30 and Central's current slot at 6.00 pm. This is a cause of great dissatisfaction to the producer who feels that this works to his disadvantage in terms of ratings, because a proper comparison cannot be made. The IBA does make the necessary weighting adjustments to compensate for the differences in transmission times, but what their calculations do not allow for is that there is a smaller number of people available to watch at earlier transmission times, and many of the potential audience are still travelling home from work.

The most popular time is the 6.30 slot and when Charles Denton shifted the transmission from 6.30 to 6.05 in January 1981, it caused an outcry from the viewers in the ATV region. The reason in ratings terms was to hammock the local news programme by showing five minutes of news headlines at six o'clock after ITN's news at 5.45 and the rest of the programme, ATV Today, at 6.30. The audience resented the change, both those who were at home who found it inconvenient in terms of their domestic duties and those who were at work for whom it became impossible to watch the programme. The change did improve the viewing figures for the news programme but it certainly did not please the Crossroads viewers. More recently, since Central took over the franchise, Crossroads has been edged back to six o'clock, again for the benefit of the news programme. The time slot for a programme is not simply the concern of the ratings; it also has an effect on the status of a programme and the way the programme-makers feel about the way their programme is received within the broadcasting industry. The viewers may adapt to the different times, and even different ways, which is evidence of the programme's popularity, but the juggling about proves that the programme is not considered worthy of a definite time slot throughout the ITV networks.

What is Crossroads about and what does it set out to achieve?

JB You see TV, the high percentage of TV today – it doesn't matter what anybody says – it's relaxation and escapism. Now if that is so and a high percentage of TV is for relaxation and escapism, who is to say, who is to scoff at what people like and dislike, fifteen million of them. And

unless somebody goes round and knocks on every door
and says why do you watch this . . .

Jack Barton is unequivocal in his aims to entertain, but there
are many stages in the production before he can achieve that
aim. It is possible to look at the production of the programme by
splitting it into separate areas and then seeing how they combine
in the end product. In Crossroads there are three processes at
work at any one time. These can be split into production management, scripts, and programme-making, and although they are
inextricably intertwined, it is easier to talk about them separately,
as long as the connections are not lost in that separation.

The overall planning of the programme is done three months
ahead and Jack Barton commented:

We have to plan three months ahead all the time. I have to
make the same decisions – sometimes that might be wrong,
turn out wrong, no good crying over spilt milk, that's it, you're
going ahead and looking all the time, not at what's gone, and
if something doesn't work for whatever reason, you say, 'It's
water under the bridge, profit from the experience.'

When the term 'production' is used about a television programme the word is not usually thought of in the same sense as,
for instance, the production of a motor car, but the speed of the
work, the multi-layered planning operations and the technical
nature of the production processes which are involved in a programme means that there are many similarities in the use of the
word. For Crossroads is in one sense produced on a production
line. There are many people involved both in technical and
administrative support and I have not considered many of these
aspects of the work because this book is not intended to be a full
production study of the programme. However, they are all vital
to the overall production and their omission is not because I do
not recognize their contribution but rather that many of the
technical skills are beyond my ability to describe adequately as
part of this book.

At the production management level there is the Crossroads
office, whose staff are permanently working for the programme.
All the day-to-day, year-to-year practical and administrative

aspects of the production are handled by the staff. Barbara Plant is Jack Barton's secretary. Margaret French's role has been mentioned earlier in this chapter, and she is in overall control of the office staff who work on the programme. Between them the office staff, Linda Bertram and Anne Clarke, handle all the records of the cast and the extras, book the auditions for the extras and cast, handle the mail and telephone calls from the audience, which is a very large part of their work, and many other day-to-day activities. There are two typists, Susan Richardson and Kay Manté, permanently employed typing scripts, and keeping records. Maggie French explained:

> So I've got two girls who type the scripts. Their job in life is purely copytyping, but the bonus for them is that they're reading the progression of stories, and in their way they contribute tremendously because they'll pick up continuity mistakes that have got through to that point. They type the storylines which come in, which have to be distributed to the writers, so they're seeing the new stories that are coming in. They do now log special events like weddings, births and so on. It became apparent that we'd really got to get some sort of organization going because it's been apparent over the years that we're being called upon more and more to produce research from years ago and your brain can only hold so much.

The atmosphere in the production office was extremely warm, friendly and co-operative, and the women who worked in there were as conscious as anybody else of the adverse criticism which was directed towards the programme. They suggested that if the IBA were seriously concerned about the audience and the programme, they might like to come and sit on the end of the phone or answer some of the letters which were received from the viewers, to find if they were satisfied with the quality of the programme.

The production of the Crossroads scripts is the work of five people: Ivor Jay the script editor, Peter Ling who prepares the storylines and the three scriptwriters who are working on the programme at any one time. Currently these are Edward Barnes, David Garfield and Arthur Schmidt. The writing of the programme is obviously a collective effort, but although the writers change, Peter Ling and Ivor Jay are clearly crucial in the overall control of the writing and for the ideas which are put into the programme.

There is a script meeting every other Tuesday and at these meetings the scripts are planned for three months ahead. Basically the ideas for the stories come from Ivor Jay:

> Well I devise all the stories. I usually do what they call the major, which is about seven or eight pages of the essentials of the story and the answers that one wants to get out of the story and then this is introduced at the script conference. It's pulled about a bit. Sometimes it goes through plain sailing. Then the story is usually – one usually has a writer in mind for it. Peter Ling then takes the major away and he breaks it down into scenes. And he keeps in touch, refers to me, and sometimes there are aspects perhaps that he's not sure about or he wants to change or whatever, and then he does this breakdown, two weeks of scenes, and before the meeting the writers each get a copy.

The outline for the major storyline is discussed by Peter Ling, all the scriptwriters, Jack Barton and Margaret French, and often details change from the original conception of the story. The following is an example of the way that Ivor Jay presents a 'major'. It is the first page of an outline for the introduction of a new character and storyline which was being planned last summer and came into the serial before Christmas.

> LAMONT
> Stripped of its nuances and variables, this is the story of a middle-aged, chauvinistic pig who falls deeply in love. And plays a waiting game sustained by the unholy alliance of hope and cynicism.
>
> Which is that the continual plying of gifts (expensive) and attentive considerations will eventually bring the bird down off the tree.
>
> The woman with whom he is in love is SHARON METCALFE.
>
> Which implies and tells us much about the man, LAMONT. And these characteristics and feelings will be explored and shaped to make, one hopes, strong and intriguing drama.

SHARON is a no-nonsense, strong-minded woman. She does not bestow her favours, sexual or platonic, easily. She's salt-of-the-earth material.

So here's the cynical womanizer in pursuit of the sceptical, unattainable lady.

Ordinarily, SHARON wouldn't give LAMONT a second look (except to register a more considered contempt).

So – plausibility has to be worked in.

Events, to begin with, must be made to bring about the continuance of an unlikely relationship.

The first meeting of SHARON and LAMONT may be a chance one and locks them both into more than a cursory 'hello-and-goodbye' because of their respective relationships with EDDIE LEE.

It may be that LAMONT has visited EDDIE recently. And, naturally, SHARON will want to know about EDDIE. She can't even know that he gave himself up. Or of the saga concerning BECKY and BARBARA.

That first meeting is critical. SHARON will show qualities (candidness, loyalty, sexuality) which will ensnare LAMONT.

LAMONT's own character needs strongly to be deepened and broadened.

He has to be invested with raffish charm (which is not at all difficult for the actor, incidentally) and strong areas of his own brand of honesties.

As for instance, with SHARON he could be entirely truthful (except on matters of, say, evidence which might send him to prison) because there are some people who can take honesty at its most disturbing and would prefer it. Others are too vulnerable. And it is kinder to sustain them with lies.

With LAMONT intentions are paramount, i.e. if the intention is good then it is okay to do a bad deed.

To simplify: murder is bad. But the intention to murder a megalomaniacal, dangerous shit, say Hitler, would be good.

This really can't be called cynical. It is, incidentally, and LAMONT wouldn't know this necessarily, the teaching of the Hindu lord, Krishna.

In LAMONT's down-to-earth amused candours such a philosophy would acquire a peculiar charm and even invest him with kindness.

Would his wife be happier if she knew of his spells of womanizing? (Actually, she does – but he doesn't know she does. 'When he bought me my first fur coat I knew, then, that there was another woman. Each time there was another woman I had another expensive present.')

His son is a policeman. To be revealed dramatically. A show-stopper of irony.

How would it benefit his son, LAMONT would blandly ask, to be told that his ever-loving dad was bent?

Sustain the lie and everybody's happy.

We need, I think, to backtrack to LAMONT's activities.

To launder the man a little.

All that we have against him at the moment is the theft of a cargo of cameras.

The rest must be accounted to rumour, gossip and malice.

Now there is in the camera business a large and profitable area known as 'grey' imports. Indeed, the largest retailer of photography equipment in the country – Jessop – make an advertising point that their prices are black and white . . . not grey. That their products have been properly imported and are covered by genuine guarantees.

Okay, now can we make it plausibly possible that the cameras which EDDIE LEE helped 'lift' for LAMONT actually belonged to LAMONT in the first place – but were grey imports?

Etc, etc . . .

The collective contributions, relating to the way that other characters would be able to react to the new character, are discussed and in fact many changes are made from the original concept.

Of course, a new storyline has to fit in with the existing threads of stories and there is also the question of where the new stories are to be physically located – will they need a new set? Once the concept is accepted it is broken down into storylines by Peter Ling, and the outline of the episodes are presented to the meetings. Each meeting discusses four episodes as well as new stories. Each episode is usually broken down into eight or ten scenes and consists of three storylines. Each writer writes one particular storyline and this aspect of Crossroads' construction is seen to be unique by Peter Ling. He feels that it gives the writers more overall control over the character development because they can carry a story through to its conclusion rather than having different writers writing complete episodes. Each storyline is written by one scriptwriter and then the episode is edited together by the script editor. The storyline breakdown which Peter Ling presents to the scriptwriters contains the outline of the story for the scriptwriters to work on. The following is an example of two scenes of a storyline breakdown.

SCENE 1 (IMPACT) THE OFFICE (8.30 PM)

Adam has been working late, and is just packing up when Barbara enters.

He is surprised to see her; he thought she was having a cosy evening at home with David. She says ruefully that that *was* the original idea – but it misfired . . . Is Meg around?

Adam says no, she's gone out: 'I'm in sole charge tonight – anything I can do?'

Barbara sighs: 'Not really. I was hoping to let off steam, that's all. David and I have a difference of opinion and I couldn't sit there all the evening, freezing to death – so I decided to get out for a change of scene.'

Gradually she confides in Adam; the sweater was a disaster – David won't even wear it. And there's an interviewer from *Silhouette* coming to talk to them both tomorrow, to make matters worse.

She did have one genuine reason for coming over to the motel tonight; now she's finished her new novel (she had the manuscript with her in a file) she wants to pack it up so it can go off to the publishers. She's going to cadge some brown paper, sticky tape, etc, and make up a parcel. Adam says he'll help her.

SCENE 2 IRIS' ROOM (8.35 PM)

Ron and Iris have clearly been having a long, romantic session together; suddenly Iris remembers she was supposed to be going to the pictures with the landlady this evening . . .

Well it's too late now – but the landlady is not going to be at all pleased.

Ron says: 'I'll explain to her – I can talk her round.'

'No, don't,' says Iris. 'That might make things worse. She's a bit funny about me entertaining men friends here – she'll probably be banging on the door soon, saying: 'Everybody out!' It'd be better if I talk to her, and apologize.'

'Tell you what – we'll see her together. After all, I am your cousin – I'm taking you out for supper – what's the harm in that?'

She looks at him lovingly: 'Are you really going to take me out? Honest?'

'Why not? We'll have a really good meal – where d'you want to go? Anywhere you like – it's up to you.'

Iris thinks, and then says, with a touch of defiance: 'Crossroads Motel . . . Yes – I'd really like that.' etc, etc.

From the breakdown scenes, and after a lot of discussion about how the characters should develop and what the main points are that have to be emphasized, the writers produce their scripts. Ivor Jay explains:

From the breakdown scenes, then they go away to write that particular scene, because each writer has a different story to follow and then two weeks later they produce their scripts which I have to edit and go through. I don't want to sound pedantic about it but there may be aspects of the scripts – there invariably are – that are, I don't like, or I don't feel have been explored properly or sensitively enough or there may be odd things that they've missed and so on and some editors like to do the rewriting themselves. I don't. I think it's the writer's story, and the more involved they get, the deeper the satisfaction if they do it. I discuss it with the writers and say there are aspects about this that I think you've gone wrong on, or I think it might be useful if you did this, or I think it's a boring theme, you know. And what I do, I have to become even more inventive and think of aspects that one might develop or introduce. I have to edit the script and give them some kind of continuity and that kind of thing, and also work with the directors in terms of I give them optional cuts because of the pacing. This is difficult to gauge, particularly the 19½-minute script is more difficult to judge than an hour's play or a 50-minute play. If a 50-minute play is three minutes under you can spread it a bit, slow paces. In a 50-minute it's lost, you see, but if it's three minutes out of 19½-minutes it's much more difficult then. It really shows.

It would be impossible to select a script which could be seen as representative of Crossroads, with the programme reaching its 3600th episode. The following is picked completely at random from the scripts which I read.

CAMERAS	SOUND	ACTION/DIALOGUE
		SCENE 3 BROWNLOWS' LOUNGE NIGHT
		Kath
		Arthur
		(6.05 pm)

Kath and Arthur come home from work together. See them in the hall taking their coats off before they come through to the lounge . . .

ARTHUR: Jenks laid it all on . . .

KATH: Tomorrow?

ARTHUR: Aye . . .

KATH: They don't give you much notice do they!

ARTHUR (*pleased with himself*): What notice do I need for a trip to Newcastle?

KATH: I only thought . . .

ARTHUR: Sit on a train – all expenses paid – couldn't give me too much of that!

He has walked into the lounge. The table has not been cleared since lunchtime.

ARTHUR (*re table*): What's all this then?

KATH: All what?

ARTHUR: That table . . .

KATH: Be our Glenda . . .

ARTHUR: Leaving it in that state?

KATH (*making it alright*): She told me about

CAMERAS   SOUND   ACTION/DIALOGUE

it – had to go back to work lunchtime –
Mr Dobson was here . . .

ARTHUR: Eh?

KATH: To see Kevin

ARTHUR: What about?

KATH: Well I don't know do I!

And she sets about clearing the table.

ARTHUR: Fool to leave that place . . .

KATH: Now don't start that again.

ARTHUR: Was. Good solid firm. Established. Nice fella Dobson.

KATH (*sarcastic*): You know him do you!

ARTHUR: Seen him about . . . Why did they
have dinner at home anyroad?

KATH: Why not – it's up to them.

ARTHUR (*dismissive*): Huh . . . I was thinking today . . . it won't be all that bad a
thing . . . to be on our own again . . .

*Shot of Kath looking across at him. She
doesn't think that. Their eyes do not meet.*

ARTHUR: Two of us . . . I'll have a scout
round for a place . . .

KATH: In a *day*?

ARTHUR: Well the *area* . . . and property's
cheaper up north . . .

KATH (*a sigh*): They're not *giving* it away,
that's for sure . . .

ARTHUR: Read it somewhere . . . could be
quids in out of this move . . . Why don't
you come with me?

KATH: Eh?

ARTHUR (*warming*): Tomorrow, for the
day . . .

KATH: You'll be busy . . .

ARTHUR: You could look round the shops
while I'm at the office – meet up, have a spot
of lunch together, give the place the once
over . . .?

CAMERAS   SOUND   ACTION/DIALOGUE

KATH (*an excuse sound*): No . . .

ARTHUR: Be a nice trip out . . .

KATH: You go on your own . . .

ARTHUR: Thought you'd have fancied that . . .

KATH: I'm working . . .

ARTHUR: Could give that a miss for one day . . .

KATH (*hesitantly*): And in the afternoon . . .

ARTHUR: *What?*

KATH: I'm supposed to be going to see Iris . . .

Close shot of Arthur's tight-lipped face.

End of scene.

The practical production of the scripts is not the only way in which the script editor is integral to the stories. For in the same sense as the producer, his ideas are integral to the themes and content of the programme. The concept of the happy ending is central to the thinking of Ivor Jay and it can be seen as part of his philosophy which appears in the programmes.

IJ   You see I'm not against glad endings, you know. I think you can dive deep and come up muddy and you get told, 'This ain't life because it's a happy ending.' A lot of things do end happily in life. And also, more importantly, I think if you hack down the endings you deny something that's basic in viewers. When you are doing a documentary or a play documentary or a one-off play, that makes you want to be profound and significant and make statements and so on, and your ending is necessarily down-beat and illogical. Okay, that's fine, but I don't think in soap opera you can go on, and I don't think realism is synonymous with sort of dejection and defeat at all, and there again you see I have a lot of respect for viewers out there and I wouldn't want to depress them, you know.

The overall message then of Crossroads is optimism, by intention, and not realism based in a depressive portrayal of everyday life.

It is written into the scripts, and the message of Crossroads is survival and the ability to overcome difficulties and learn from the problems which are encountered along the way.

It is a message which is needed by those who work on the programme. The difficulties which they have to overcome are many. Aspects of a production which are normally not a problem become so for those working on Crossroads. The work of the designer can be taken as an example. When I spoke to Norman Smith, who was one of the original designers on the programme, he told me that one of the basic difficulties which the designer has is that he is designing sets which may be for one storyline and yet be there for many years and have to be adapted for many different stories. Many of the sets have to be multi-purpose, providing locations for different characters and storylines. However the main problem for the designers is that they are not fully aware of how the storylines will develop before they have to begin working on the sets. Normally a designer has a completed script for a dramatic production before the set has to be designed. They often have met the cast for whom they are designing a living location and can incorporate character features from the performer into the choice of furnishings and fittings which are included in the set. This is rarely possible in Crossroads although 'Meg's sitting-room' had apparently been decorated in colours which suited the colouring of the character as well as reflecting her character tastes. Designers work closely with directors, but because there are three directors working all the time on Crossroads, the designers may design a set for the first week that a character appears in the serial which suits the artistic requirements of that director, then, two weeks later, another director who is working with the designer may find the set totally unrealistic for his concept of the character. Crossroads is not a programme where anyone can indulge their artistic preferences; everything is produced to the service of the overall programme. Each week's three episodes are required to take place within the physical locations of the six sets which it is possible to locate in the studio area. Similarly, if a new set is being designed, then its physical dimensions have to be such that they can fit in with existing sets. Peter Ling has to make sure that the storylines can be fitted into the sets which are available at any one time on the studio floor. Writing and designing for Crossroads may not enable those involved to practise their artistic craft to their personal satisfaction, but they certainly have to be very artful in managing to create at all against such overwhelming restrictions.

The three directors working on Crossroads at any one time all work on a three-week cycle with two weeks' preparation time. During these two weeks they read the three scripts, which are colour coded – the green, the yellow and the pink – prepare their own camera scripts and see designers and other technical staff who are involved in the production. During the third week of their cycle they are responsible for directing the three episodes. Some directors have worked on the programme for many years, some stay for a relatively short period of one or two years. Often freelance directors work on the programme on a regular basis. ATV/Central staff directors sometimes may direct two or three episodes when they are moving between finishing one production and beginning something new. The directors all have different styles or ways of working and it is certainly possible to detect variations in different programmes if you have watched them long enough to distinguish a director's particular style. However, Crossroads is not a programme where a director can give a programme his or her individual style to any great extent, because the format and time available does not allow for many personal indulgences. Although I spoke to many of the directors who had worked on the programme, I specifically followed one director, Mike Holgate, through various weeks of productions to gain an overall picture of the director's part in the programme. The speed of turn round on Crossroads is particularly difficult for directors because although they are not pressurized during the first two weeks of their cycle, when they get to the studio there is so little time available that they invariably end their week's work dissatisfied with the standard of their episodes. When a director receives the script, he has to work out how he is going to make the performers move around within the sets while they are saying their lines, and how he is going to arrange his cameras to cover their moves and tell the story visually while they tell it verbally. Mike explained:

MH   I think that's what makes Crossroads interesting. It's the movement. Because the script is usually fairly limp, so if you actually get people – conflict arises with people's moves – do you know what I'm saying – and if you can get good shots then I think it backs up the script because the script is usually very flat. So if you can actually get people moving . . .

DH   The script isn't really indicating whether they should move or not?

MH   Not at all, no, no. I mean I just get a virgin script which has nothing on it at all. It sometimes has on stage directions, which will state what the artist should be doing at the time, but it won't necessarily say where they should be going or what they should be doing and I think a lot of television is that. I will get very bored watching something that is very static, if you see two people sitting down. Unless the dialogue is so scintillating that it holds you and grips you, unless they're doing something, then I think it's very mundane and flat. Okay, so that's the biggest problem, sitting down by myself and actually thinking what they will do and how they will react and why they should react. The other thing I do is cut the script. Ivor Jay goes away and puts in optional cuts which he wants, you've seen . . . Okay, so I will put my own cuts in as well.

Apart from working out his camera moves, the director also has to liaise with the designer for the week about how the sets are to be arranged on the studio floor.

On the Thursday of the second week the director has a production meeting. Here the designer presents the plan of how the sets will be constructed on the studio floor, and the cameras, sound, and lighting departments all comment on how the plan will affect their ability to work on the production. This meeting is essentially for discussions and to sort out all the problems which might arise *before* the production goes into the studio on the Thursday and Friday of the following week.

MH   The designer has done a plan of how he and I think the sets will fit in. They are different sizes as you can see, they fit in different ways and they have to be fitted in a way that will help lighting as well because they have to be fitted on what we call flylines which are where the lighting tracks are, so they can't be set any way. At the meeting we have sound and cameras, and they will say, 'Oh yes, but if you have that there then I can't get my boom in,' and then cameras will say, 'Well it'll be hard for cameras because they can't do that.' I know myself, I know the problems that they have, but it's much better if they see the problems themselves as well because they feel that they're making a contribution and it doesn't mean that I'm just going in and saying, 'Well that's it, and do it, lads.' Because everybody's problems are different and really you can't account for everybody's problems when you're trying to work out one set of problems at a time. The important thing is to make sure the sets fit, because they're all different shapes and sizes, so once you've done that then you go away and it's quite easy to revise a set and it's much better to revise it once you've talked to cameras and sound otherwise you might have missed something. And it's also quite important to sort out as many problems as you can beforehand, especially on something like Crossroads where the time factor is the most important element. I mean when something goes through smoothly on the day, it's because you've gone away and done your homework and made sure that it will all work. The most embarrassing thing is when you go into a studio on a recording day and you get cameras with cables crossed. I mean it's happened to me before, you know, and you think, 'Oh shit, I should have worked that out before.' It's happened, it's got to, of course. There are so many differences and imponderables.

If the director has done 'all his homework' and allowed for the many 'imponderables' that might arise, then everything is ready for the week's rehearsals to begin on the Monday morning, to turn the next three episodes into the finished programmes.

CHAPTER 4

Inside the Motel

You just haven't got time, the whole thing is just pressure, pressure – finish on time and get it done.

A Crossroads director

Every Monday morning, the director for the week, his production assistant (PA), and the stage manager arrive at the rehearsal rooms in a large office block in one of the least inspiring industrial areas of Birmingham. The glamour of show business is not reflected in the rehearsal room where the cast begin arriving before ten o'clock for the week's work. For make no mistake, appearing and working on the production of Crossroads bears little resemblance to the glamorous world of theatre or light entertainment, or even the relatively short situation comedy series which may run for six weeks.

The rehearsal room is far from similar to ATV Studio 1 where the recordings take place on Thursday and Friday, and so, before the cast arrive, the stage manager for the week, Liz Stern or Harold Wolfenden, has the job of constructing mock sets with tables, chairs, old sofas, beds and innumerable objects with which the performers play 'let's pretend', in accordance with the requirements of the script. The rehearsal room is not 'taped' or marked out to represent the sets which will appear in the studio and the performers have to work within the limits of the imaginary sets, which do not relate accurately to the actual sizing of the sets in the studios. Of course, the 'regulars' have grown accustomed to the sets, but for new performers it can be quite a shock not to know exactly where they will be sitting, standing, moving to, etc.

The rehearsal rooms are divided into two discrete areas: the large room where the rehearsals take place; and a small kitchen where the cast can make tea or coffee during the day, with a room furnished with easy chairs and sofas, where the cast spend their time between their scenes. It may be comfortable in a sparse

kind of manner, but it affords absolutely no privacy and the cast
remain in very close proximity with one another throughout the
three days which they spend there each week. Sometimes they
just chat to each other, but most of the time they go over lines
and get ready for their scenes. Sometimes they share jokes;
sometimes, inevitably, they have little moans about the scripts;
but it was a very friendly and relaxed atmosphere throughout the
time that I spent there. Of course, it has to be, for in such
confined space it would be impossible for everyone should any
animosity break out, and it must be a very difficult situation to
be working in. The cast are thrown together and part of the
necessary qualifications to survive in Crossroads is the ability to
be accepted by the other members of the cast. The group close-
ness which has developed over the months or years of working
together is a bonus for those working on the production but, of
course, it can present a problem for new artistes and even for
new directors. It is an obstacle which has to be overcome and it
is a natural part of any group working closely together, but with
the added pressures of working at such speed, it could add to the
tension which inevitably exists. It is rather a case of all being in
the same boat together, only some people have been in it a lot
longer and learned the survival techniques, and others are simply
going along for a short cruise. This is not a criticism of the
performers, but an explanation of their 'hold' and involvement
with the programme. In fact, they are very helpful to newcomers
when the performance begins, because, inevitably, any weakness
which may come to light is a reflection also on their own performance, and no one wants to look weak because of the weakness
of a co-performer.

The call for the beginning of the first rehearsal, designated by
the colour-coded scripts, starts the week, when the stage manager
calls the cast from their 'sitting-room' into the rehearsal room.
The rehearsal begins straight away, for there is no 'read through'
when initial problems or queries can be ironed out. Instead the
cast act their first attempts at the episode for the director of the
week. This is a fascinating part of the rehearsal. Here the performers can give their initial reaction to the script. Some lines
they may find unsatisfactory, unconvincing, or just simply ludicrous. Lines which may appear at first glance to be innocuous

are played to reveal double entendres or bizarre 'jokey' meanings. The resulting performance appears more like an episode of Soap than Crossroads and reveals the thin line between the serious and the 'send–up' versions of soap opera. The process has various effects. It is initially a way of relaxing the performers who can make the transition from the 'real' into the performance which they are acting. More importantly, it is also a signal of lines or even words which could well be problematic if they are left in the finished programme. Sometimes the words are changed and sometimes the lines are cut. Often Mike had already spotted the 'problems' and was ready to cut them before they were pointed out to him by the performers. To be fair to the scriptwriters, often it was only when the lines were read by the performers that they appeared ludicrous, sometimes because of the interaction between performers, who played off each other to reveal the humorous possibilities behind the script. The problem arises if they are not meant to be funny. Sometimes the lines were left in but it did appear that this initial reaction by performers and director was often a very good indication of areas of the script which were not very good and the programme benefitted when they were cut. It was clear, in fact, that the performers and director are, in this sense, reacting in the way that the audience may react to dubious lines.

When I was watching the rehearsals during the summer, Mike was relatively new to directing the programme and although he reacted against faults or weaknesses in the script, he did sometimes put the passages back in when 'time' demanded it. 'Time' is essential in Crossroads, as in all television productions, and throughout the rehearsals, from Monday through to the actual recording, at every point, the production assistant is timing each scene or part of a scene to ensure that at the end of the day the complete programme lasts for $19\frac{1}{2}$ minutes. Sometimes a passage was cut and then if the overall timing was 'under' it had to be re-inserted into the script. However, by the end of the year when I was watching again, he was much more confident and cut lines completely according to his discretion, and if he felt that it was to the benefit of the finished product.

MH   I will cut things if I think that the dialogue is padding or if it adds nothing to the scene, or if it slows the scene up, especially the beginning and the end. I'll always cut things at the beginning if I think that it's delaying what the scene's about. There's always a hook to the scene, you'll always read a scene and you'll decide there's something in that scene which should be – do you know what I mean? – which should be grabbed.

Mike was here expanding a cut he had made which he saw as 'waffle' because the script took a long time to get to the point, but in actual fact it was a more serious error. The script was referring to something which the audience did not know about and it appeared not to make sense to him. One advantage which the director has is that he is able to make cuts in addition to the optional cuts provided by the script editor and this is more freedom than is normally afforded to directors because the writers are not ever-present to defend their lines or complain. Mike continued:

MH It's editing. It's only editing in the sense, I'm not even worried now about how the episodes will run, whether it'll under run or whatever. I just cut what I think is waffle, then I'll worry about putting in stuff afterwards. And I'd rather put in moves, you know, to make up the time.

DH Like in the summer when there were things you were cutting out and then sometimes they had to go back because of time?

MH Yeah, but I've learnt now, that's the other thing, that after a while you learn you don't just put things back because they are . . .

DH Because of the time?

MH Because of the time, unless they're stating anything. I mean I think I'm one of the few people that do this but some directors will just put stuff back, you know, just to pad, but I don't think that's right. I'd much rather put in a move and have somebody doing something, which I think is much better than having people saying things that don't mean anything.

A second level at which the cast act as their own scriptwriters is that they pick out lines or information which they may feel is incorrect in terms of actions which they have performed in earlier scripts. Sometimes these are actions where they feel they may be acting 'out of character'. If it is not possible for these points to be decided on by the director and the cast, they discuss them with the producer before any final changes are made. Similarly, a member of the cast may say, 'I said this same line last week,' but in most cases this is a deliberate repetition for the audience. The scriptwriters know that viewers do not always see or even 'catch' every line of dialogue, and there is a need for internal referencing and bringing up to date within the serial. As far as the director is concerned, he has to decide whether any of the comments from the cast will 'improve' the programme or needs investigating and he needs to keep the rehearsals moving and not waste too much time in discussions.

After agreeing the cuts which he plans to make, the director continues with the rehearsal. The performers may rehearse a scene two or three times, maybe four times until both he and particularly the cast are relatively happy with the scenes. Mike explained what he wanted from the first day's rehearsal:

DH   So when the exciting day comes on a Monday morning, tell me about that.

MH   Well, I always find Mondays are very 'Mondayish' anyway, because they are like, they are Monday, so that's the problem you have. But it's also gearing people up to try to get them enthusiastic, because they've just finished a week, another week, and they come in and it's fresh and they've usually only looked at the script once over the weekend, which I think is probably fair enough really, because I mean you need two days break. So what I tend to do on the Monday is to get people to move where I want them to be, so I get that instilled in their brains, and I get the script workable, so that at the end of the Monday I know that (a) they know where they're going, what they're doing and why they're doing it on the set, and (b) that the script is okay, that they can learn the lines and that they understand what they're saying and why they're saying it. They're quite important things really, these sorts of problems. So that all those kind of things, so they're very sort of vaguish, you know, no they're not vaguish, they're kind of the framework that you work to so on the Tuesday you come in and hopefully everybody will have learned their lines so they'll be able to work without script and then you can start working on performances and motivation and why people should be doing what they're doing and the way they should be doing it and the inflections and everything else.

As Mike indicates, from the point of view of the performers it is not possible to begin learning the scripts perfectly until after the first day's rehearsal. Partly there has not been enough time since they have only finished the previous week's recording on Friday evening at around 8 pm and many of the cast travel home at the weekends, which is often not in Birmingham. More importantly, it is better for them to wait until any changes have been made during Monday's rehearsal because they may have to 'unlearn' lines which are cut. In this context, it was mentioned to me that visiting performers often found difficulty in 'unlearning' scripts which they had learned before the first rehearsals.

Despite the pressure under which they work, by the time that Thursday and Friday come round the cast all do know their lines and I saw no evidence that performers did not know their lines. In fact, accusations to this effect seem to be part of the unsubstantiated attacks made against the programme. Of course, occasionally someone may stumble or momentarily forget a line but this is no different from other productions which I have watched. The difference is rather that in a studio recording of a situation comedy series, if a performer forgets a line then the 'warm-up' man will often make a joke of it with the audience if the scene has to begin again. In drama productions the scene would simply be shot again. Sometimes the performer may be using a style of acting, trying to attain a form of 'naturalness' or 'conversational tone' and not appear to be reciting written lines. It may be that some lines are difficult to learn or deliver but that would appear to be a fault in writing rather than performing. Often, such lines or maybe just words would be changed if it were possible without altering the sense too drastically.

The restrictions of preparing camera scripts before seeing the rehearsal was something which I intially thought would be more of a problem than it seemed ultimately to be. However, there appeared to be a limited number of camera positions which could be used because of the close confines of the sets and the restrictions did not seem to cause as many problems as I had originally envisaged. In most productions, the director will rehearse for a couple of days and then go away and prepare his camera script after seeing how the actors are performing and what the performance looks like in rehearsal. But this is not the way that the directors work on Crossroads. Although most of the camera shots and moves had been worked out before coming to rehearsal, it was not until the director saw how things would look when the actors said the lines that he could begin to assess how his camera script was going to work out in the studio. The actors need to know how they are going actually to move on the set as much as they need to know their lines, and that is something which the director has to work out in relation to where he knows his cameras will be and what shots or pictures they will be able to take.

MH   Actors need to know what they're doing and why they're doing it. So once they've done that, then they can go away on a Monday night and they can think about that, you know. It's something mundane like peeling potatoes or filling a kettle or anything, you know, provided they know that they should be doing that and that they should have stopped filling the kettle and they should turn for the next line. That is fairly important in their minds, and also I think that, varying on the weeks, I mean most actors have either a lot to do or a little to do and if they have a lot to do the more they do on a Monday the better it is for their own peace of mind.

While the performers may have been assured what their moves will be they can go away and learn their lines, but the director may find that he has to go away and rethink his camera shots.

MH   Sometimes you just want to give up, then you just go away and say, 'Let's all go away and come back the next day and re-think it.' That's sometimes quite a good idea as well.

The Monday I go away and re-think a lot of things. That's quite interesting in that you can actually see the conflict of how you originally thought a scene would work and then when you see it, when you actually hear them saying the lines, then it becomes apparent that it won't work in the way you thought it would, which is quite an eye-opener sometimes. So then you go away and you re-think the whole thing. It doesn't happen with every scene but it happens with some scenes, so then you go away and come back the following day and re-do it the new way.

On a Tuesday you come in with a lot more confidence and a lot more zest and everyone has had a good night's sleep. Tuesday is the better day really. It's a more satisfying day because that's when the little nuances come out of the script. Then you can actually work on things and where possible the actors will contribute a bit more because they will have thought about the lines a bit more as well and they will suggest ways of improving or trimming things that they will say. So it's a much more creative kind of day, do you know what I mean in that sense? In terms of the text. So, hopefully, at the end of the Tuesday you've got something sort of vaguely workable.

Mike's comments reveal his calm, patient attitude and his willingness to adapt and change the way that he had first thought of directing the week's episodes. This ability to be flexible and to make adjustments to original thoughts is particularly necessary for directors working on Crossroads, because nothing can be finally planned and changes are desirable if the programme is to look interesting in visual terms. Young or new directors bring an enthusiasm to the programme and their desire to make the programme 'better than its own reputation' is recognizable. One director who was no longer working on the programme, however, reveals the differing attitudes which are felt in response to the amount of work which is necessary to make the end result look good:

I think perhaps a drama director has no place in Crossroads, and it's funny, I find my response to directing them has changed, having done it for a long time and sort of tried to treat every scene as a little cameo, and then gone away and done things that are certainly more reasonable, and that one can take more pride in, I find that I came back to it with a totally different attitude. Much less desire to put my mark on it. And I think that's the fault of young directors, who say, 'I'm doing Crossroads and it's a step up for me, so I'm going to make it really good so people will notice me,' and in fact all they do is notice the silly shots or that Meg is curiously subdued. I think the answer is just to tell the story simply and let them play it, because they know it better than you do. Obviously if something is going ludicrously over the top you put it right. I think the trouble is, you see, that the guidelines are set down by the fact that anyone involved in Crossroads is either on the way up or on the way down and not at the top. So you either get very tired directing by numbers which turns up quite a lot, or you get someone knocking his pan out for no reason. But nobody quite serves the show the way they should do. I don't know how you do serve the show.

By Tuesday evening the episodes are beginning to take more shape and then the director has to prepare the amendments to his final camera script and the production assistant has to retype them so that they are ready for Thursday morning in the studio.

Wednesday is the last day of outside rehearsals. On Wednesday morning the performers run straight through the three episodes for the benefit of the technical staff who will be working on the programme in the studios on Thursday and Friday. The technical staff who attend the run should consist of the designer, the head cameraman, lighting and sound staff, wardrobe, and the floor managers. The floor manager is the person who is in control in the studio on recording days and his or her job is to relay the director's instructions and requests to the performers and other staff. At the rehearsal the floor manager takes the function of giving the performers their cues and controlling the action. This is the first time that the director can stand back and watch the performance objectively, and make any changes before the afternoon run-through for the producer.

Since Crossroads has a limited arrangement of sets and most

of the people who work at ATV are familiar with the programme, few problems usually present themselves at this rehearsal. However, it is essential that everyone attend the rehearsal and there was a tendency for familiarity with the programme to lead to some people not always turning up. It must be stressed, it was a minute percentage, but nevertheless this could and did lead to problems in the studio on occasions when I was there. It was an example of the attitude towards the programme which prevailed with some people within ATV – what might be described as the 'It's only Crossroads so why bother' syndrome. It was an attitude which added to the difficulties with which the production already had to deal in terms of their time schedules, for the programme needs absolute commitment from its technical departments if it is to keep to its production times. This was a problem commented on by many members of the production team but the implications are much more serious when it comes to the recording days.

The rehearsal on Wednesday morning is usually over quite early and the cast go back to the studios for lunch. Although the rehearsal rooms are located away from the studios the cast and production staff move between the two sites from Monday to Wednesday. They go back for lunch and usually return there after rehearsals finish at around 5.30 to have their evening meal. At this level they are thrown together socially as well as working together and Jack Barton is part of the social group. They eat together and talk in the canteen, and some spend evenings together. Many of the cast do not live in Birmingham, travelling in on Monday mornings and returning to their homes on Friday nights. Most established members of the cast have permanent homes in Birmingham even if only during the week, but performers who are in the cast for a limited period and staying in hotels or 'digs' spend a lot of their time together. In this sense the producer spends a lot of time with the cast, is very involved with them and always knows what has happened at rehearsals, but his official visit is the Wednesday afternoon producer's run.

Wednesday afternoon at two o'clock sharp, Jack Barton arrives in a taxi from the studios for the producer's run. This is the rehearsal where both the artistes and the director perform for the producer. The atmosphere is one of expectancy and slight tension. The nearest analogy I could use to describe the mood of the experience is to liken it to the headmaster, teacher and pupil relationship in a friendly comprehensive school. Certainly the afternoon has a special atmosphere and the feeling of an event, and it is Jack Barton's attitude to the cast as much as anything else which colours and creates the atmosphere. There is a seriousness about the performance and Jack watches with apparent detachment, although not without recognition and approval if the performance satisfies him. He deliberately maintains a rather stern exterior so that the performers do not get slack or complacent about their performance. I could see that to sustain a long-running series this was an understandable tactic in maintaining a sense of commitment and pace. I found the mood rather tense, very much one of a performance for the producer, and at the end Jack Barton did congratulate and give his approval.

The producer's run is also the first time that the director can stand back and watch the performance without actually having to 'direct'. All the directions and cues are given by the stage manager who will be working on the studio floor on the Thursday and Friday.

MH   On the Wednesday afternoon I can stand back without scripts and I can be fairly objective and I can just watch the performance and how I think it will work. I forget about scripts and cameras and everything else and I just stand and watch it and sometimes I find things quite useful come out of that, little things that you just miss will come out of that last run.

DH   And do they ever change, does Jack ever change things or say things that will be totally different?

MH   Rarely, rarely. He will sometimes – the hardest thing with Jack is if you have a new character come in and if the director isn't briefed well enough on how the character should be, or what the character should be. I mean a lot of the time I guess it's down to the director to find out, you know, how this character should play the part and how he should react to certain people and other people, so that probably the producer can be the overseer. He can come in and say, 'Well I think the character in six weeks time will end up at such and such a point, so I think now he should be playing a lot more lightly or he should be a lot heavier.' Because I think the director of the week is a bit blinkered really, because he's not really too concerned with the next week or the week after that, so you tend to give notes that relate to the script as you see it and as you read it. Okay, well it might not necessarily correspond with what happens next week or the week after that.

DH   So you don't really know what's going on in the future.

MH   Not really, no. I mean I don't read scripts all the time, I don't read all the scripts. I read my own scripts. I read storylines.

Here Mike is pinpointing the overall control which the producer holds over the production in terms of his knowledge of the forthcoming stories and character developments. It is also more than simply 'knowing what it is going on', it is a sense of the producer having more power than the director, and the cast did seem to approach the producer rather more than approach the directors with problems. This is natural since the directors are only working on episodes once every third week, but it does tend to block, to a certain extent, the development of close cast and director relations. For the directors do not have any power in the production, it is only the producer who has the power to hire, fire, and develop a character to continue for any length of time in the serial. It is also, of course, a matter of the social relations which the producer has with the cast. Much of their free time is spent together, as explained above, and they do develop a closer relationship with Jack than they do with the directors.

At the end of the producer's run the cast have finished for the day and this is the only day when they are likely to have an early finish. When I was there Noele Gordon explained that late Wednesday afternoon was one of the only times when they could arrange hairdressing appointments, dental appointments and so on, and guarantee that they would be able to get there. However, for the director the day is not finished, for he and the producer return to the offices and the studios to check that everything is ready for the recording days on Thursday and Friday.

For the director this means going down on to the studio floor and checking that the sets have been erected and generally looking around to see that everything looks as he would expect it to. Sometimes it is only possible to visualize certain camera shots which might have been envisaged when they are seen *in situ* on the studio floor. Often something which had looked relatively simple on a camera script can turn into a difficult problem which will potentially hold up the studio for too long the next day. One such incident occurred when I was with Mike, who had a scene which was to take place between Miss Luke and the young boy who had attacked her. He came to her cottage to inquire how Benny was, and the scene was written to take place with her opening the door but keeping it on the chain which she had had fitted after she had been attacked. She was to appear on one side of the door, with Len, the boy, appearing on the outside, and the scene had to be shot from either side of the door. The chain which was on the door was not long enough to allow the camera to see the other character through the opening and a longer, more flexible chain had to be made and fitted to enable the scene to be shot. Last minute checks have to be made because when the production starts work on Thursday morning, there is little time for any problems to be sorted out.

DH   Let's talk about studio days. (. . .) What is a studio day for you?

MH   When I've arrived at the studio I relax a little bit because I think that by that stage I've done enough to make sure that it works, and then if it doesn't work then I've only got myself to blame for not having done any work on the previous three days. So in theory the studio days should be nice and relaxed, that's the theory. But then you have other problems to contend with like flares (lighting problems), like cameras not working and like shots not working. (. . .)

     The first half hour on a Thursday is very slow, the first hour really *is* slow, the whole of Thursday morning is slow, come to that, and you never get the same performances I don't think on a Thursday morning as you get on a Friday evening. I always think my last episodes are better and I don't know whether that's because you've

had two days and everyone is well oiled, I suspect that's
it really.

Studio days are a very interesting example of the meeting of
two different work cultures in television production. The studio
staff – vision mixer, cameramen, lighting and sound engineers,
recording staff, scenery and props department, etc – spend all
their working time in the studios, but the production team and
the performers only spend two days a week in the studio, and in
the case of Crossroads, the director is only there every three
weeks. There can be a different attitude to recording sessions by
the two different work groups and the main function of the
director is to foster and maintain good relations and create enthusiastic working relationships. Of course, at the end of the
day, what the director needs is for his programme to be completed, on video-tape, ready for transmission in three weeks time,
but the journey from 9.30 Thursday morning until 8.00 on Friday
evening can be either troublefree, along a straight fast motorway,
or very slow and painful along meandering country lanes, sometimes without benefit of a scenic route. This process is what
Mike calls 'that sort of obstacle to get over – just getting everybody to get into a groove and working well'.

Actually, it is not just getting them working well, it is keeping
them working over the next two days, and with the attitudes
which prevail towards Crossroads within the company, this is not
an easy task. In the following extract, Mike explains the mixture
of professional attitudes to productions:

> In studio the important thing really is just getting a nice
> atmosphere. If you get that, then you're half way there – if
> you get a nice working atmosphere and if you radiate the kind
> of confidence and people think that you know what you're doing,
> then that helps as well. Most people are quite professional in
> their attitudes and they like to see a programme done well
> even though their name might not be on the end of it, they
> still like to say, 'Oh I work on that.' And they like to think
> that the whole thing is quite good and quite well directed be-
> cause it rubs off on them, cameramen and whoever, and if it's
> not well directed and if it looks bad and shoddy then they go
> away thinking that they haven't done anything they can enjoy

watching. I mean the nicest compliment is to go into the bar at the end of the day and the cameraman to say, 'Hey, that was great,' you know, and really to have enjoyed working on it. And sometimes they do and you know that they'll go away in two or three weeks time and watch it at home, and actually enjoy watching it. So you've got a responsibility to make other people feel that they're involved and feel that they're contributing.

In a long-running serial like Crossroads keeping a high level of adrenalin flowing for every recording is a very demanding task. The problem is particular to such forms of drama. It is not a problem in the short six-part situation comedies where they have the combination of the studio audience and the atmosphere of a theatrical event to help carry the performers and production team through the recording. Neither do the cast or production team in Crossroads have the luxury of the facilities available to a single play where there is time to correct performances and edit after the recording session.

It is wrong to make generalizations about Crossroads because although each week's production schedule is basically the same, the short time allowed for the recording means that any combination of circumstances can affect the recording of a week's episodes. In order that the cast and production team can achieve the best effect with the material and resources available, they need the technical conditions to work without a hitch. This is not always possible, even with the best intentions.

The current format of Crossroads, with three episodes per week, means that one and a half episodes are recorded each day. At the end of Friday night what matters is that the three episodes are completed, because if they are not the repercussions for the production are very serious. This is the constant pressure which permeates the whole of the two days' work. Part one of the green script is recorded by Thursday lunchtime, part two of the green and part one of the yellow on Thursday evening, part two of the yellow on Friday morning and parts one and two of the pink on Friday evening. Each section has to keep to the alloted time otherwise the remaining sections lose time.

There are various locations at the ATV/Central studios which are all used when the programme is being rehearsed and recorded. At a very basic level they can be split into the studio, the control rooms and the recording areas. The studio is where the sets are erected by the scenery department and all the sets are then 'dressed' with appropriate props for each scene. This is where the actors perform their parts and the cameras and microphones transmit the picture and sound to the control rooms above. The floor managers are responsible for discipline on the studio floor and for transmitting the instructions from the director to the performers and anyone else involved in the studio. The camera and sound operators are in direct two-way communication with the control rooms.

The main control room is the location of the director, his PA and the vision mixer. The director sees the pictures each of the four cameras is showing on a series of monitors in front of him. His production assistant calls the shots, i.e. tells the camera operators which camera's picture is at any time being recorded, and which camera they will be coming to next. Each camera operator knows which shot number belongs to him and how the action is being covered. The PA also times every scene as it runs throughout the rehearsals during the day and during the recording, and if scenes over- or under-run then the time has to be adjusted in another scene. The vision mixer is the person who physically selects the pictures electronically which the director choses.

To the left and adjacent to the main control room is the sound control room where the sound supervisor and the grams operator sit. To the director's right is the vision control room where the vision engineer and the lighting director and lighting console operator sit. Tele-cine is the area from which any filmed material which is to be included in the programme is 'run' and recorded in with the action which is being recorded from the studios. The whole programme is recorded in 'VT' by the videotape technician and it is he who has to make any edits or 'joins' in separate parts or scenes of the programme.

During the long days – 9.30 am to 8.00 pm – the cast, when they are not actually on the studio floor, are either in their dressing-rooms, or waiting in the small waiting areas between their dressing-rooms and the studios, or in the canteen. As at rehearsals, much of their time is spent together but at least they do have the privacy of their dressing-rooms to retire to. Throughout the day, the producer is ubiquitously overseeing the proceedings and Ivor Jay is also available to judge and assist if necessary.

The first rehearsal begins at 9.30 and this is when the director sees what the first episode looks like through the cameras, as opposed to seeing the actors on the floor in front of him, when he had to imagine what his planned camera shots would look like. The cast begin the first run through, and the moves which have been rehearsed in the mock sets in the rehearsal rooms are tested to see whether they work in the real sets. This first run through can take a very long time, with many re-runs of very short passages of dialogue or physical movements while the director makes sure that the shots which he has worked out are giving the pictures he wants. This is the time when the floor manager is vitally important and his or her job is not only transmitting the instructions of the director to the cast, but also, crucially, re-assuring the performers and keeping them happy during what are often very long breaks while camera moves are worked out and shots changed. Since there are a limited number of people who can hear what is going on in the control room, there are a lot of people on the studio floor for whom this part of rehearsals is a slow, boring and possibly alienating experience. The performers survive this by joking and chatting, although everything they say is overheard by the people in the control rooms upstairs. But for the scenery and props department, who have to sit around all day until they are needed, it can be a very boring experience. This is where floor managers can sparkle and inspire, or destroy the day. They are never insignificant, for it is their mood and skill which carries the whole performance through. The floor manager more than anyone else creates the atmosphere on the studio floor. The majority of floor managers whom I watched at Crossroads were very efficient and certainly aided the director and kept the cast and staff happy and working well. However, if a director on Crossroads happens to come up against a floor manager who is 'not having a very good day', the effects can be disastrous. One floor manager I watched managed to alienate the camera operators, transmit the feeling to the studio floor that the director did not know what he was doing, when the director was in complete control and showing no signs of stress or anger, and have the actors coming out of the studio asking, 'What's going on?' A more flamboyant or aggressive director would never have tolerated the situation, but with the control which the floor manager has it is a brave director who would have a showdown with a floor manager during the middle of a recording day. I must stress that this was an isolated incident, but Crossroads does not have the time to absorb any such incidents. Everyone has to be committed all of the time.

When the camera rehearsal is completed, the call is given for the dress run and after a short break for the performers to get ready the dress rehearsal of the first part of the first episode is performed. During the dress rehearsal, the producer, the script editor and the other two directors working on the programme all watch in the producer's room and make their own comments and notes on the performance. This is an interesting experience because the directors are making comments about each other's work in a way which I have not seen on other productions. They all watch the performance and make comments for changes or improvements, although these are usually quite small. At the end of the rehearsal, the producer goes up to the control gallery and gives his notes and suggestions to the director. There is then a call for notes to be given to the performers and everyone gathers down in the viewing room for the director to give the notes. Often these are quite slight, like 'put in an extra beat (pause) after a certain line' or, for instance to David Moran (Kevin Banks), 'Can you look out to the camera when Lynette (Glenda) is saying that line because I am taking a reaction shot of you.' They are normally points telling the performers about the way the camera is recording the action, or technique points about the acting. If there is anything wrong with a performance it is also mentioned, but Mike told me that if he had any serious personal acting notes to give to a performer he would give them privately or ask the floor manager to tell them privately. I have never seen public notes given to performers in other productions and although it could be seen as a little nerve-racking, it does seem to have the effect of psychologically preparing the performers for the recording which follows immediately afterwards.

Time flies on and the recording usually begins with a limited amount of time available, always too little. The first half of episode one has to be 'in the can' by 1.45 on Thursday lunchtime to keep to the schedule. Morning recordings are not usually a problem because they have only had to do a half episode, but when the evening session comes round and there are two parts to be recorded, time becomes much more of an ogre.

The same process of camera rehearsal, dress rehearsal and recording session continues on the Thursday evening and on Friday morning, until the first two episodes are recorded. Of course, no two recording sessions are exactly the same, but they are very similar. By Friday afternoon, when the production resumes after the lunch break, usually at 3.00, the director has his last episode to record. If they have got ahead on the Friday morning, he may have managed to begin his camera rehearsal; if not then it begins after lunch and with luck everything progresses without a hitch until the early evening when the recording takes place. Whatever time it begins, the recording session has to finish at 8.00 prompt and it is then that the speed of the turn round really catches up with the production. If everything goes well then, of course, there is no problem, but it is virtually impossible for an episode to go without any hitches and each time the recording has to stop it creates a problem for the timing which is so restricted. Sometimes, when I watched recording sessions, the actual performance which had been worked on during the week at rehearsals was lost as the time progressed and the director had to make an instant decision as to whether to let a 'slip' go through, or even a performance which he knew was less than the performer was capable of, because he knew that if he stopped and re-recorded a scene he might have to speed up at the end or else run out of time.

The irony of working on Crossroads is that the more effort a director puts into his week's work, and the more complex or interesting he has attempted to make the episode, the more likely he is to run into time problems during his recording days. One of the episodes which I watched Mike direct had a kitchen scene with a lot of frantic activity and a storyline which involved a row breaking out between members of the staff which quickly spread to the whole kitchen staff, finally exploded in crashing plates and overall chaos. It was fast, exciting and amusing. When Mike came face to face with the complexities of directing it in the studio, while it worked perfectly, it took a long time out of his

working day and that meant that he had to forego some interesting effects which he had planned for the end of the episode.

In another episode there were scenes when Benny was visiting
the eye specialist after he had been injured in a car accident. The
incident had been researched, a nurse from the eye department
of a local hospital came in as advisor and all the correct ophthalmic
equipment was borrowed for the episode. The lighting director
made a special effort to create the correct lighting conditions for
someone who was being examined after such an eye injury and
the scene was very dramatic, well acted and effective. Again,
however, it took a long time, and Crossroads cannot afford the
time that such scenes take. Watching the production on studio
days it is easy to see why it is possible to adopt an attitude of
getting through as quickly and simply as possible because the
more adventurous a director is with his shots or the more complicated the action is, the more problems he sets up for himself,
and the more chance he has of being dissatisfied with the complete episode.

Crossroads could employ the method of rehearse-record, which
means that the director would have his camera rehearsal for the
complete episode or half episode, and then each scene would be
rehearsed followed by the recording of that scene. This is the
usual method employed in television drama. However, this depends on the availability of post-production editing facilities,
which are not available to Crossroads. Even with the system that
they use, of recording the complete episode, editing facilities
would vastly improve the programme and alleviate some of the
pressures involved in its production.

Crossroads is a very low-budget production and this is perhaps
the over-riding factor in the final look and quality of the programme. The effect is quite simply that the production team
have to work within a budget which does not allow them the
luxury of facilities which are taken for granted in other productions. The most crucial facility which is not available to the programme is that of post-production editing, which is the means
by which the director has a day or even half a day in a video-
editing suite, with a video-tape editor, after the programme has
been recorded. This means that any errors can be edited out of
the tape and a general standard of 'professional finish' applied to

the final version of a programme. The effects of this facility are not simply in terms of the correction of errors; it does have many effects during the actual recording of the programme. Because of the necessity to keep the programme to a strict time schedule there are constant problems of timing during the re- cording. This means that if the timing of, for instance, scene 2, runs over its allotted time, the director has to decide, during the recording, at the same time as he is directing his crew and per- formers, which part of the script can be speeded up to catch up with the time which has been lost. In these circumstances, the director is at the mercy of his performers being able to speed up their delivery and not affect their performance. In the case of the episodes which I watched, the director was aware of those performers who could speed up or slow down without it affecting their performance but it was not something that he could ask of visiting actors or actresses who were not so familiar with the workings of the programme.

However, the more serious effects of the lack of these facilities is in terms of any slight mistakes which may occur during a recording. If a performer forgets her or his lines, then obviously the production has to stop to enable them to take a prompt and get back into the character and point in the plot. The director now has to take a decision as to whether to go back to the begin- ning of the scene and make an edit or whether to try to make an edit using the Editec facility at the point where the stop has occurred. This latter course is itself time-consuming – on average an edit took about eight minutes – and can result in more tension for the performers while the technical edit is made. Sometimes it is not successful and then the process has to be repeated. In one instance when I was watching the recording, an actor made a slip on one of his lines and as his tension increased he repeated the slip, so that the time taken to get the line correct ate into the recording time. Had the director had post-production editing facilities he could have simply continued from the original slip without the time spent going back to a convenient editing point.

Without the ability to edit a director cannot improve the pro- gramme after the recording is finished. Normally when any drama is produced the director can look at the programme and make any improvements which he might feel are needed. Often the most effective reaction shots – that is, shots of one or more characters reacting to the dialogue of another character – are taken separately by the director, while the actors who are 're-acting' perform the expression for the cameras. The director then inserts the shots during the editing session. If a director on Crossroads is taking a reaction shot, he has to take the person talking on one camera, and everyone else has to hold their expressions for the length of time it might take him to switch to one or more cameras for different shots of other re-actions. All these are small points, but overall they do affect the finished programme and its standard of production, which is criticized.

It seems unlikely that this editing facility will be given to the programme, since when I asked Charles Denton why it was not available he said that it was simply a question of cost and it was not possible to give it to the programme.

DH The thing that amazed me most when I watched it was that it didn't have post-production editing, which would make an amazing difference to it as far as I could see. Why have you never given it that?

CD Because it's not an economic job to actually give it two days editing or whatever it is.

DH Well it would only take a day, wouldn't it?

CD A pretty expensive thing though when you have 156 episodes a year. The economics of a soap opera like that don't allow for that sort of post-production method. Over a week you would run out of time, you wouldn't be able to do three.

DH Well why do you then feel that the economics of the programme like that are so much different to the econo-mics of other programmes?

CD Well we don't do anything else that runs 156 times a year. It's on, it's part of the foundation stone of television weekdays in this country – and Coronation Street. You don't actually have a better programme necessarily. You only have a different financial foundation stone for the rest of the evening. You probably have a show which you probably can't afford to keep on having 156 times a year.

You are coming back to two a week and that isn't what the game's about. The game ought to be about having five a week.

The reasons why the money is not available must be seen not only in relation to the amount of money for productions but the priorities which determine how that money is allocated. It is one thing to say that because the programme is produced throughout the year it cannot have a bigger budget, but it is necessary to ask *why* certain programmes are seen to warrant larger budgets, and in the case of Crossroads *why* it is not seen as necessary to provide more money to improve its standards. When the programme is criticized for its 'professional standards' by those critics within the broadcasting institutions, they are well aware that the professional *technical* standard could easily be improved by the simple injection of funds into the production. That the controller of ATV does not see the need to inject extra money into Crossroads does reflect his attitude to the programme, the genre, and the audience. Technical improvements cost money and as Charles Denton says, 'If the programme were improved in this sense it would not necessarily get more viewers.' He is not alone; soap operas are not high in the ratings when the television companies allocate funds. But Crossroads is the most cost effective form of drama on television.

The whole production cycle of Crossroads is the combined effort of many different people, and the speed of turn round makes the programme unique in British television. A soap opera can only really be judged in comparison with other soaps and it is unfair to make comparisons with other programmes. As the director for the week completes the last episode on Friday night, the cast leave for the weekend with the next week's scripts to learn. Soon it will be Monday morning and they will be back at the rehearsal rooms ready to start again.

CHAPTER 5

Performers, Characters and the Audience

DH How much is David Hunter Ronnie Allen?

RA Remarkably little if you are talking about actual personalities, remarkably little. But then how do you divide personality from appearance? I look the same way and I talk more or less the same way. Those things are the important part of what personality is really like, but the character qualities are very, very different indeed.

For the television audience the main attractions of Crossroads are the stories and the characters who appear in the serial. For some people the performers and the characters whom they play are inseparable and there is a complete fusing of the two identities. The audience tends to think that they 'know' the character even though they do not actually have personal acquaintance with the performer. This seems to be particularly prevalent in long-running series like Crossroads or Coronation Street where the actress or actor is often not seen by the television audience in roles other than in the serial. Audiences do not simply see characters as stereotypes, nor do they necessarily see performers as being typecast, but they do see the performers as possessing the qualities of the fictional character whom they portray. This is not surprising since it is the effect which the creators of fictional representations set out to achieve. Some critics are amazed when the public believe in a character, but the performers are well aware that their job is to create that illusion. Ronnie Allen who plays David Hunter readily understands the relationship between his own character and that of the part he plays, as perceived by the audience:

As I said before, it's part of my job to make them believe that David Hunter exists, but I actually don't care whether they know that Ronnie Allen exists. In fact I always try to avoid publicity. Interviews I avoid whenever I can because I prefer to be an actor playing a part. If they take me for real, that's the part.

The creation of a fictional character is a combination of many contributions from various members of the production team and performers. The original idea for a character comes from the script editor, Ivor Jay, who produces a character outline and the first storyline in which the character will participate. The storyline is developed through the scripts and the actual casting for the character is not done until quite late in the proceedings. In this sense when the artistes are originally cast in a part, they are cast to suit the part as it is written, but if they stay in the series there are character changes which are developed to take on board the characteristics of the performer, and contribute to the fusing of the two identities.

Portraying fictional characters is the work of an actress or actor, but often it is harder to play someone who is actually supposed to be ordinary, without outstanding characteristics, than to portray a strongly-written character. One reason why the characters appear as 'realistic' to the audience is because to a certain extent they see them as having the same qualities as the star. Although the public may see Noele Gordon as synonymous with Meg Richardson, the actress sees the situation quite differently;

NG   It's just playing a part. I mean Meg Richardson is no more like Noele Gordon than the man in the moon.

However, this statement is not without its contradictions. What I think she means is that the *personality* of the actress is nothing like that of the character she portrays, but certainly the outward appearance of the character very closely resembles that of the actress. This is a deliberate facet of the construction of the programme. The performers are given a clothing allowance for their character and are expected to buy clothes to suit. When I was there, Lynette McMorrough bought three blouses from Marks & Spencer which she called 'Glenda blouses'. Noele Gordon told me how she chose clothes to suit the character of Meg Mortimer:

NG   You see I never wear anything too extreme. You look at
     some clothes on television – the light entertainment side
     of it – and think, 'Oh, that's stunning, but of course, I
     could never wear that.' I've always been very careful not to
     wear anything too extreme or have too extreme hairstyles,
     you know, so that people think, 'Oh well, I can look like
     that,' you know, which I think is a great thing . . .

Noele Gordon may carefully avoid extremes or excesses as befits
the 'reality' of Meg Mortimer, yet since she selects the clothes
for the character, they do reflect her own tastes.

DH   Do you choose what you wear most or all the time?
NG   Oh, yes, we provide all our own clothes. Except for any-
     thing unusual like a wedding dress, or when it's a question
     of men, evening dress or morning dress, anything unusual
     like that is provided. And uniforms like waitress uniforms
     and things like that.
DH   So it's really up to you what you wear?
NG   Yes.

This freedom is not as total as it sounds because the producer
does have absolute control over what the performers finally wear
for the recordings and he did exercise a certain amount of veto
over what they wore if he felt that the clothes were not 'in
character'.

When I was watching the recordings in the summer, Kathy
Staff, who plays Doris Luke, had a scene where she had to visit
the specialist who was treating Benny in hospital and instead of
wearing her normal drab raincoat, the actress dressed in the character's best coat and hat. At the end of the dress rehearsal Jack
Barton insisted that she wear her everyday clothes, although in
this case the actress seemed correct in her assessment of the way
the character would dress, based on her knowledge of the way
that women 'like Doris' would behave in 'real life'. After the
incident, I asked Kathy if she had the same overall freedom to
choose the clothes she wore:

DH   Other actors have said that they choose what they wear
     and how they look, is that the same –
KS   No, not really, not for Doris. I mean Jack is very strong

on his feelings of how Doris should look and he will not allow me to wear any jewellery whatsoever. No jewellery at all, not even a watch, and when I went to see the specialist I put on the coat that I went to the ballet in, because I think Doris would have brought out her best coat and her best hat to go to see a specialist at the hospital. I mean, to me Doris would put that on when she's going to church and when she was going to see a specialist. But of course then, you see, when I do wear things like that, Jack said I looked too good so therefore he made me change and I had to put the old raincoat on and the hat which is quite good, but I still don't feel Doris would ever go to visit the hospital in her old raincoat which she goes to work in.

DH   I agree, that sort of woman definitely wouldn't. That's one of the only things she would dress up for.

KS   Well, she doesn't go out too often and she keeps her clothes probably five, ten years so they'd be old fashioned but then they'd be in good condition and she would wear them on those special occasions. So I can't honestly say that I am allowed to dress the character as – a lot of the time I am, but there again I'm in an overall and the black, and when I'm at the farm I'm in what I wear at work because I'm always working.

So I don't have a lot of choice really to dress the character. I mean, even for Glenda's wedding I asked could I have my hair set in a simple style, but just, 'Oh no, no, no, no like this,' and that's it. He won't move from that. That's why I have to keep my hair this length, because if I have it any shorter it's not long enough to go up in the roll, so I have to have it in a longer style so that I can do that for Doris because he won't change, he won't move on that at all. I don't mind because I believe that she is a bit of an old-fashioned character, but as you say I do feel on special occasions she would.

The need to make the characters look ordinary or everyday also needs to be followed through in their mode of dress, and Pamela Vezey and Lynette McMorrough, who play Kath

Brownlow and her daughter, Glenda, are examples of parts where the actresses are slightly different, at least in class terms, from the characters whom they are playing, although they both said that the characters had taken on board some of their own characteristics. In terms of 'dressing down' to a character they were conscious that the producer had, to a certain extent, kept control of their appearance. Pamela Vezey told of one incident:

PV   Yes, he told us once I think when we all looked too nice. We looked like sort of adverts. He said we all looked terribly fresh, you know, as if – but it just happened that we had a crisp blouse on, but it comes over, especially blues. They come up very bright, you know. But apart from that it's just what we've got really.

It is obviously easier for performers whose own personality more closely resembles the character in the serial to make choices of their own without comment from the producer. Both Ronnie Allen and Sue Lloyd, who play David and Barbara Hunter, did merge aspects of their own style into their choice of clothes for the characters they played.

RA   Well actually that *is* character, the actual appearance and the clothes. That's the character, although they are my choice. It was established when he first came into the show that he was going to be a very clothes-conscious man, who again – partly it's his business interests – regards running a motel very much as being a public relations job. Therefore the staff and the management have got to look good and appealing to the public. So he was originally a very clothes-conscious and appearance-conscious man. I am not particularly.

Actually, Ronnie Allen may not be clothes-conscious in relation to the 'smart suit' appearance of David Hunter, but his personal dress style is equally well chosen and casually tasteful, and there are elements of style common to the character and the actor. Similarly, Sue Lloyd, although denying that she was as smart as Barbara Hunter, did recognize aspects of her own clothes style in the clothes she chose for the character.

DH   Do you buy clothes for the Barbara Hunter character?

SL   Oh yes I do.

DH   Is that different from Sue Lloyd?

SL   Oh very much so. I am far more casual than Barbara
      Hunter. (. . .) But I've always been cast for elegant clothes
      and things like that.

DH   But Barbara Hunter's elegance is not 'straight', it's not
      conventional elegance. It's much more a reflection of
      Sue Lloyd's . . .

SL   That's right. Absolutely. I have a flamboyance . . . I sup-
      pose I bring a lot of myself or my thoughts on elegance
      into it, which is slightly different, slightly bizzare. She is
      not slotted into a Sloane Ranger type.

The construction of character through dress and appearance is
an aspect of fictional representation to which audiences respond
most readily. Just as we 'read' the style and personality of people
we know through their dress, so the physical appearance of the
performers is the first visual clue to their character. The women
and men to whom I have spoken were quick to comment on
Noele Gordon's appearance in the serial, but it is as Noele
Gordon the *actress* and not the character she plays about whom
they think they are speaking. It is her hairstyle, clothes, bearing,
make-up that they talk about, always in a favourable manner.
The audience readily comment on the appearance of performers
and criticize them if they do not reach the standards they expect
from them, as a character. Clothes reflect personality and the
change of personality can be signalled through changes in the
clothes that a character wears. Performers can try to make subtle
changes in their own character clothes as a means of changing
their personality and the producer told me that he has to monitor
these changes. He believes that all the performers want to play
'good' characters, even if they start off as a 'bad' character, because the audience more readily responds to 'good' characters. If
the performers start changing their own dress style in a way that
changes the character, then the producer has to veto it. He keeps
the cast in their character as it is written and prevents them
changing the character before the script warrants any changes.

The performers have also introduced their own personal
preferences into the characterization. Originally instituted as a

means whereby the performers act as their own script editors, it has had the effect of fusing personal characteristics of the performers with those of the characters they play. Noele Gordon explained:

NG   It is virtually impossible for a script editor to keep tabs on every character and every storyline – very difficult. So in a way through all the years we've had to be our own script editors. When we started we decided that the easiest thing to do was to bring in our own preferences, our own personal preferences, so that it would keep us straight. For instance, I don't eat sugar, so you never see me taking sugar on screen. And I don't drink whisky and I don't drink gin, so you never see me having a scotch or a gin on the show.

DH   Do you think it's better that you can do it yourself?

NG   Yes, because again you see, our writers change, they are not aware of previous storylines, that go back years and years and years.

DH   Does that give you more control over what you are doing?

NG   Well, I think it give us more control over the reality of what we are doing, yes.

Similarly, Tony Adams, who plays Adam Chance, has a personal interest in boats and owns a large boat. The character in the series, Adam, has an interest in boats and this is a part of the storyline. In this sense the characterization builds on the reality of the performers and contributes towards the 'reality' of the series. The viewers' knowledge of this fusing of interests is often brought about by factors external to the programme. Actors and actresses are always newsworthy with the popular press and stories of their personal lives, loves, likes and dislikes abound. Television viewers are also newspaper readers and the information which they gather from various media sources is fused to provide a much more comprehensive idea of performers and characters than that which they 'read' in the programme.

There is, however, much more to the merging of personal characteristics of the performers and the parts which they play within the serial. The scriptwriters actually pick up the personal mannerisms, attitudes and speech patterns of the performers and incorporate them into the personality of the character whom they are portraying. Carolyn Jones who plays Sharon Metcalfe, the secretary in the motel garage explained:

> You get a devious practice whereby the scriptwriters get to know you as well, they watch you and of course they're going to take your qualities and you suddenly find yourself saying what you may have said yourself, or having attitudes to people that you have in real life.

Sue Lloyd also explained how the character whom she plays has developed from the original storyline, when she came into the series, to her current role as the wife of David Hunter, an interesting character in her own right. Her story is typical of characters who are introduced in a relatively minor way but then develop into more substantial characters within the serial, and it illustrates the merging of the qualities which the performer brings to the part and the way the writers capitalize on the personality of the performer to incorporate them into the scripts.

SL   Well I came in to do only ten weeks originally, when I met Jack Barton, when I came in to discuss the part. I came in as a writer, which I am now anyway. I came in to do some research work and I took this job on as a housekeeper because I was going to do a story about how a doctor would react to poisoning. It was all very obscure, the whole thing. And I was mixed up with the doctor, Dr Farnum, and then I met David Hunter in the period of time and they just thought that he was due for another romance. He hadn't had one for a few years, so, er, I was the right height, so . . .

DH   So you didn't expect to be staying when you first came in.

SL   No I didn't. I expected to be in for ten weeks, and go off again. (. . .)

DH   So how much do you feel that the way you play Barbara is now – I mean is it you?

SL   I've settled it back to myself, yes. Yes, she's very different to when I first came in because when I first came in, oh it was very sort of wafting here and wafting there, then a sort of affair. Very unrealistic.

DH   You lived with Dr Munroe, didn't you?

SL   Yes, that's right. Yes, and I was definitely playing a part and I think that sometimes happens when people come in for a short time. They are playing a part which is slightly unrealistic.

She continued explaining that the writers wait to see what characteristics the performers possess and then incorporate them into the scripts.

They might take certain qualities which you might have but which they seem to find out for themselves, which is extraordinary ... It's a slight likeness and of course they use that in some of their storylines.

One of the directors also confirmed that the scriptwriters incorporated these personal characteristics into the scripts, even at the level of stage directions. One actress, when she joined the cast, had normal stage directions for her entrance as 'X enters room, etc'. After watching the actress's natural entrances, the stage directions changed to 'X sweeps in'.

It appears then that many established characters in Crossroads do possess characteristics which are based, at least, on the reality of the performers and this must have the effect of making the characters appear 'real' to the audience. Of course, this fusing of performers and characters cannot work with all characterization since some of the characters do not have very much in common with the actor or actress who acts the part and in those cases there is a different relationship to the audience. Such a case is Paul Henry, who plays Benny Hawkins in the series. Benny can be described as educationally sub-normal and Paul Henry has definite views about the character he plays and how he chooses to play it.

PH   He's not as bad as he was at the beginning, for the simple reason that there is no way I could play a lot of the stuff with that type of mentality. I think he has improved as well as he possibly could, as now he can hold conversations and he can communicate, basically because of the attention he has had.

He has developed the character himself and improved the capacity of Benny, for his own professional satisfaction. Certainly, to watch Paul Henry at rehearsal, the script was not much more than a guide, for he changed many lines, retaining the sense, but making the character appear a little less inarticulate. He explained:

> PH   It gets to the point, you see, that you know more of the character than the scriptwriter does and I think basically because they are working as quickly as we are, that they give us an idea and we put a bit of it into our own words.

However, it must be said that Paul Henry was more likely to make these changes, almost as a matter of course, than other performers and the result was much better than the original scripted version. Paul Henry feels that he has a great deal of freedom in playing the character of Benny, precisely because there is less public expectation, based on prior knowledge on the part of the audience, to which he has to conform.

> PH   I mean, I love the character. I can swing from the ceiling, I can cry, I can laugh. I mean, acting is about emotions, there are so many emotions and you can use them to certain degrees, where with a character like Benny, he can go to the extreme on every emotion and as long as it is based on a certain reality, he can get away with it.

However, he does have a delicate job to perform when appearing as himself in public situations where he is billed as 'Paul Henry, Benny from Crossroads'. Because he is playing an educationally sub-normal boy, he is partly a figure of fun, but also one with whom members of the audience who are themselves disabled can identify. His following includes children who are themselves mentally retarded and who see the actor very definitely as the character whom he plays.

> PH   I get a lot of spastic children that, say if I have done fetes and . . . There's one little girl that comes everywhere that I am and she really believes in me and it wouldn't matter if I was standing there with a crown on, I am still Benny to her.

And another story he told:

> I have got a friend in Grimsby who works with the fish and
> there is a lad on the docks who was always very insignificant,
> who was just like a piece of rag, didn't exist. Now they all call
> him Benny and he's chuffed – because suddenly he's identi-
> fied, you know. So I suppose Benny in a lot of ways sort of
> helps the people like him to get an identity.

The character of Benny is one which is subject to much criticism and disparaging comments. However, 'Benny' is part of
contemporary folk language – to mention the name is sufficient
to evoke a response, often humorous, from viewers and even those
who profess never to watch the series. Benny is, for the most
part, held in affection by his audience; critics may mock the
character but it is perhaps the only attempt to represent a
mentally-handicapped person in fictional terms on television. It
would have been easy to write the character out of the series but
the production has sustained the character and is to be respected
for that. Similarly the representation of the character Sandy
Richardson as permanently crippled after a motor accident was a
definite inclusion of a physically-handicapped young man, which
enabled many socially-motivated stories to be included in the
scripts. These characters may draw criticism from various quar-
ters but they are praised by the organizations representing
disabled people, and the relationship of the actors with the
disabled in their audience is a positive one.

The merging of styles and personal characteristics of the performers into the fictional characters is obviously one of the major
ways in which the 'reality' of the characters is achieved. Even
when the performer thinks that they are nothing like the character
that they are playing there are still attitudes and mannerisms
which they have and which are used by the scriptwriters. In a
sense, the performers have a lot of control over their characters
and they do question some of the actions and words which they
are expected to say in the series, saying, 'I wouldn't do this,' or,
'I wouldn't say this,' and they do, with the co-operation of the
directors, contribute greatly to the finished characterization. Of
course, it does have its disadvantages, and it means that the

director has to tread a fine line to make sure that they do not 'take over' the character at the expense of the script, but the performers who have been in the serial for a long time are often in a strong position for 'knowing' their character. They are also aware that the level of characterization in soap opera has to be near to 'ordinary' or 'normal' people so that the audience can believe in them. As Kathy Staff said:

> In a soap opera they've got to see people that they can believe in and relate to, either the daughter, the mother, their cousin, brother. They've got to be believable people so that is why you can't really do anybody too outrageous.

Nothing causes more comment and amazement on the part of the critics of a programme like Crossroads than reports that some of the viewers actually confuse fictional characters and the performers who play the parts. No one knows more about the area of 'confusion' than the performers who are on the receiving end of the attentions of the audience. At one level there are the majority of viewers who know that the performers are acting a part and who treat them as actors and actresses, but there are others who appear actually to 'believe' in the fictional characters.

Many viewers treat the performers as performers, giving them the usual attention which is afforded to those who appear in any television programme. The attention which they receive is through letters – fan mail – and from actually encountering the public in the street. All the actors talked about this contact with the public and for the most part they welcomed it and saw it as a mark of their popularity. Ronnie Allen talked about the attention which he received:

RA They stop you in the street, you know, because actors get far more of that sort of contact, for obvious reasons. You are immediately recognizable, so we do get very much more of personal contact.

DH And do they talk to you then in terms of a fictional character or the actor?

RA That varies enormously, as much as the fan mail does, you know. Often, yes, as the real character, often they talk very sensibly, charmingly, as though you were an actor, which indeed is true, just doing an actor's job. But there are those horrendous stories about people taking it for real. We have had actors assaulted, physically, you know. They can be terribly rude, they can get aggressive.

The threats and abuse are, it appears, usually in reaction to the fictional character. There are stories about other soap operas which tell that the 'bad' characters who treat 'good' characters badly in the programme are then attacked verbally by the public when they go about their own everyday lives. Some of these may be exaggerated but there is certainly an element of truth in them. In fact, Jack Barton told me that when a young performer comes into the series and is about to play a 'bad' character, or to be part of a storyline which portrays them as acting in a way which might be disagreed with by the viewers, then they must be prepared for the adverse attention which they may receive in their contact with the public. One young actress who was considering having an abortion in the serial was refused service by an assistant in Birmingham's most prestigious department store! Long-standing stars can be the subject of what would appear to be sexual jealousy on the part of some of the viewers. Tony Adams told of how he received letters threatening physical violence to rid him of his attractiveness to women. Of course, attacks of this nature are common to everyone who is in the public eye and not specific to characters in soap opera, but what is interesting is that it is as the character whom they play that the performers are threatened, not as themselves. Conversely, Paul Henry, who plays Benny, told me that he has never had a 'bad' fan letter, nor received any threats or abusive letters or approaches from the public. Interestingly, Paul Henry does not look like the character whom he plays and is obviously 'playing a part', and there would appear to be no connection between the performer and the character whom he plays when he goes about his life as Paul Henry.

Part of the credibility of the characters and the situations in which they find themselves is determined by the familiarity of the setting or locations for the events which take place in Crossroads. The sets have become so familiar and established as 'real' locations that there is a sense in which some of the audience do believe that the cast are acting but at a real motel. Noele Gordon commented:

NG   They write to me with their problems and a lot of them write to me for jobs, very sincerely. And a lot of them write and ask me to, you know, book them into the motel.

DH   You see that's the bit I can't understand – people believing it exists to that extent.

NG   But they do. You see I mean not long ago a little old lady arrived in our audience relations office and quite genuinely said that she had come to inquire the rates at the Crossroads Motel because she wanted to treat herself to a fortnight there in the summer and they didn't know what to say to her because they didn't want to disillusion her.

DH   I wonder if they believe it exists but that you act there.

NG   I think they do. I think perhaps they do. That there is a place that we film it in.

This is not surprising, for the use of everyday settings, such as motels, streets, hospital wards, or neighbourhoods which are the locations of soap operas means that the programmes do have a reality established through their naturalness and familiarity to the audience. Of course, these arguments can be made for any plays or dramas which use modern everyday settings, but it is the repetition of the appearances, week after week, year after year, which reinforces the illusion that these places do exist. Indeed, in many cases they do, for the outside location filming is done in the 'real world' and then expertly mixed into the studio scenes. Jack Barton explained why he thought that some of his audience believed that the motel actually existed. He said that when the ITV strike was on in 1979 many people contacted the studios and radio programmes to find out what was happening at 'the motel'.

DH   You said to me that the reason you knew that some people thought the motel existed came home to you when the strike was on. Can you just explain that for me?

JB   Yes, and this again cuts across all classes. It's not people that are less intelligent than others. We who work in the industry tend to, we're so *au fait* with it, we tend to assume everybody knows, and in fact we're weaving spells in this industry, whether it be a theatre or TV, you're taking them into a fantasy land, you see, and you mustn't forget that. And therefore very intelligent people of all classes wanted to know what was happening at the motel. They knew there was a strike on and that the film men weren't filming it, but they wanted to know what is happening whilst it's still going on. So as far as they're concerned, a motel does exist, it simply had film cameras there showing us what was going on.

DH And that your actors go there and use it? I mean, they still think, they know that Noele is an actress, they know that Ronnie's an actor, but they think that they go there?

JB Yes. The press tells them they're actors and when they look in their *TV Times* and *Radio Times*, they look and see they're actors, but they don't accept it. These people really are in that motel and work out their whole lives there, and they only go home at the weekend, like taking a weekend off. They are not actors, this is not a play they are watching. This is a glimpse into a real live motel and what goes on there and how those people who work there behave, and they are not actors, and if they see them in the street, it's because they've taken an hour off from the motel and they're out doing shopping. Unless they are closely associated with those actors, but the mass of people regard them not as actors but regard them as the characters.

DH But they know –

JB Yes, but they get confused between . . .

DH I think they actually carry on that game, they play a game, they know they're playing it. It's a fantasy game.

This is an area of audience reaction which I do not pretend fully to understand. Maybe it is the 'weaving of spells in a fantasy land' as Jack Barton describes it, because this after all is one of the aims of drama. However, I do think that he is completely wrong when he says that 'the mass of people regard them not as actors but regard them as characters.' I think that the mass of people do know that they are actors and it is a small minority who may see them solely as the fictional characters. However, the reactions which some of the cast have received from the audience have definitely been at the level of fantasy firmly rooted in the everyday problems of daily life. Some incidents were humorous and some more serious. Kathy Staff told me a story of an incident which she had experienced. When I spoke to her the current storyline was the one where she had been attacked by two young men, and she had received 'get well' cards from the viewers.

KS   I had get well cards because I had been beaten up, you see. People believe that you are really ill and send get well cards and things.

DH   I think that's really quite interesting but I don't know how you work out why they do.

KS   They absolutely believe in it. They believe we are true characters and we have a motel here and that I work in the kitchen and that I also look after Benny and they believe that this is my job.

DH   So they don't think of you as an actress at all?

KS   No.

DH   What do they think when they see you on Open All Hours (a BBC situation comedy)?

KS   I think a lot of people like that . . . I don't know, they don't even recognize you because you do look different to a certain extent and it probably doesn't even register, you see, that you are the same character. It is something that psychologists really could tell you more about than I could. But we do get these letters all the time from people who really believe it. Well, I mean, about that storyline when I took Shughie to the ballet – well, he took me – and I repaired his shirts because I believed he had a lady friend, if you remember, and I turned his collar and cuffs. Well, then I got a lovely big parcel and I thought someone had sent me a present and it was a gentleman and he said, 'You made Shughie McPhee so happy when you turned his collars and cuffs and I wondered if you would do mine.' And he sent me a parcel of his old shirts. He really did, you know. You see we get it all the time.

However, there are aspects of viewers' reactions which do not come from elderly people which are even more difficult to understand. Ronnie Allen told me that he receives mail which is written to him as David Hunter, the owner of the Crossroads Motel, asking him for work at the motel and giving details of the applicant's experience. He had received one such letter on the day that I interviewed him and this illustrated the merging of reality and fiction in the attitude of the writer to the television programme. The writer was asking for a job at the motel, explained that he was unemployed, aged twenty-nine, and anxious to find work as a garage mechanic. He assured Mr Hunter that he was fully qualified in his trade but said that he realized that to appear on a television programme he would need to join Equity and was quite willing to do so. The letter was well written and appeared genuine but revealed a merging of realities which is difficult to understand.

RA   This is very, very typical, the sort of thing I get a lot of, and it's a wonderful example of how the audience look at us – this fascinating combination of fact and fiction.

DH   Yes.

RA   So that's a very typical letter. It's by no means exceptional. The curious thing is that they realize it's a fiction but at the same time treat it as if it's absolutely real, you know.

DH   When you get a letter like that, I mean, what do you do about it?

RA   I've had many of them. I don't know what to think about it. In some ways it's a compliment. After all, our job, I mean whatever we're doing, whether it's stage, theatre, cinema, or what, is to make them believe that what we're doing is real. I mean, that's our job, so from that point of view it is a great compliment, but one worries a little bit about the people themselves who can get so confused between reality and non-reality. It's a dangerous area.

One explanation may be that the writers are seeking the possibility of working at the motel in the capacity which they see extras 'working' on the sets. Certainly, there are often walk-on parts for kitchen staff or waitresses, and when people write in for jobs at the motel it is conceivable that they think that the extras are simply people who work at the actual motel and so write for jobs in the same way that they would write to any other prospective employer. In the current economic climate the desperation of the many people who are unemployed means that writing to a television company for work is understandable, if futile.

Equally interesting is the way that the production policy determines the way that performers and the production team reply to the letters which confuse the fictional for reality, for they never disillusion the viewers but go along with the belief that the motel actually exists. This policy stands whether it is the office staff who answer the telephone calls, who have to ascertain whether the caller is playing a game with them or is a genuine caller who believes in the programme. One interesting point was made by a secretary in the production office who observed that even those viewers who professed actually to believe in the Crossroads Motel knew that they had to telephone the ATV studios in order to inquire about it. Jack Barton's policy is that if the viewers who write or telephone about the programme actually do believe that it is real, then it is not his job to destroy the illusion which he has created. Whether the reactions are because television has created the 'fantasy dreams' which Jack Barton suggests or whether the audience is joining in a game and they know that they are doing it, as I suggested to him, I cannot say, but it is certainly an element of soap operas which does not leave everyone feeling at ease with the power of the genre.

However, the blurring of reality and fiction in the minds of the minority of viewers is an indication of the fine line of distinction which exists between the two areas. Since the production has set out to create that blurring of the edges in terms of the incorporation of the characteristics of the performers into the fictional characters, in a sense there is a mixing of fiction and reality in the characters who appear on the screen. It would not be likely that such confusion would occur if the programme were not deliberately operating within this area. Since some viewers actually believe in the reality of the fiction it is perfectly understandable that many more can see how closely the fiction resembles reality.

CHAPTER 6

Everything Stops for Crossroads –
Watching with the Audience

I watched it last night in colour because we had our dinner
early. I says to you, 'I'm going to be done by six o'clock
tonight,' and we had an early tea. I always used to watch
Crossroads in colour but I don't now because it's on at a time
. . . I very often watch the first ten minutes or so on the black
and white and then go and watch the second half in colour.

June

Well, I must admit when the programme altered, I altered my
tea time, because I don't want my husband to come in (. . .)
but we brought our dinner forward about ten minutes so that
we are either eating it, or occasionally, depending on what
we've had, we have sometimes just about finished and we dive
in here to watch all of it in colour.

Sheila

This chapter is about the viewers who watch Crossroads. It is
written from different sources but it is all based on talking to
people about the programme, and watching the programme with
viewers. The data comes from interviews and observations which
I made while watching episodes, and long unstructured conversations which we had after the programmes had finished. It is
important to stress that the interviews were unstructured because
I wanted the viewers to determine what was interesting or what
they noticed, or liked, or disliked about the programme and specifically about the episodes which we had watched. I hoped that
they would indicate the reasons for the popularity of the programme and also areas where they may have been critical. When
a programme has fifteen million viewers it is, of course, not
possible to speak to more than a minute percentage of those
viewers. Different people watch television programmes for different reasons, and make different 'readings' of those pro-

grammes, and much of what they say is determined by pre-conceived ideas and opinions which they bring to a programme. The message is not solely in the 'text' but can be changed or 'worked on' by the audience as they make their own interpretation of a programme.

Extracts from transcripts of interviews can appear very bland and unexciting. To *listen* to tapes is an entirely different experience from *reading* short extracts which lose, above all, the intonation and laughter of the speakers. The enthusiasm which some of the viewers have shown in their own recounting of story-lines of the programme and incidents involved in the programme can only be realized by the reader if my words are able to recreate the atmosphere of the times when I have watched the programme with them. Many asides and jokes which were made during the transmission of a programme were important indications of how the viewers reacted to certain aspects of the programme. If this aspect of the viewing experience is lost in my own storytelling it would be a great pity and I can only signal that this is an area which is important when considering the way that people watch television. Although these comments are specifically about Crossroads, there are aspects of the viewing situation which are common to the way the audience watch all programmes and talk about them.

Everyone is a television critic but most of us do not get paid for making selections and commenting upon them for the rest of the population. Using language to express opinions about artistic or fictional artefacts is a common ability, but what the speaker says about, for instance, a television programme is affected by his or her linguistic competence. A viewer who has not been trained in the conventions of literary or media criticism is not likely to use terms like 'narrative structure', 'flat or round characters', or talk about 'messages inscribed in the text', neither are they likely to be faint-hearted about using the terms 'reality', or 'true to life'. Nevertheless, they do operate with sharp critical faculties which are based in commonsense learned from their own experiences in their everyday lives and their often long experience as television critics making their own self-selection of programmes.

This book is not a suitable site for long explanations of the academic research techniques and the theoretical principles on which it is based, nevertheless some explanation may be helpful. I began the project with the idea of linking the understanding of the production process of specific episodes or programmes with the audience reception and understanding of those same episodes or programmes. Although I have gone out to watch specific episodes and to talk about those episodes, the viewers have quickly moved the conversation to the programme in general and talked about other episodes through the medium of the storylines. This has not only been the case when I have watched Crossroads but also whenever I have watched other fictional programmes, whether they are drama series or situation comedies. I always began asking about the programme which we had just watched but quite quickly the women and their families began talking about the characters by name, and moved the conversations to the areas which most interested them.

The usual criticism which is made of any research which involves the intrusion into the privacy of a natural situation is that the presence of the researcher changes the situation. This is of course perfectly correct and the researcher, far from being neutral in the research situation, does affect that situation. In fact, the interaction between the interviewer and interviewee is an integral part of the research. However, since many of the viewers talked about programmes which they had seen when I was not there, nor did they know that months or years ahead they would be talking about them, it can be said that the effect which those programmes had had upon their audience had not been affected by my presence. In fact, it became clear through the process of the study that the audience do not watch programmes as separate or individual items, nor even as types of programmes, but rather that they build up an understanding of themes over a much wider range of programmes and length of time of viewing.

I hope that the interaction which I had with those people whom I interviewed will be revealed in the transcripts, but one aspect of the effect which I had on the viewing situation does deserve separate comment. I found that my presence did not *inhibit* the comments of the viewers but rather seemed to *sharpen the aware-ness* with which they watched the programmes. A common opening comment which they made was, 'Well, it's been disappointing tonight . . .' or, 'Well, it wasn't so good tonight.' It was clearly not that the episodes were any different from other episodes, but to watch them knowing that they were going to answer questions or talk about the programme afterwards did mean that they were more critical of the episodes than they might have been if they had watched them without me. Yet when I asked why they had not enjoyed the episode, the reply was usually in terms of the characters who they had wanted to appear or at the level of there not being 'anything very much happening' in the episode. No one made any criticism of a technical nature nor did they notice any of the technical problems which I had watched being coped with a few weeks earlier in the studio.

The viewers of Crossroads are well aware that the critics for the most part do not like the programme. To ask viewers why they persist in watching a programme which has a reputation for being 'not very good' is to ask them to examine and admit why they are willing to stake their opinions against those of recognized critics or so-called 'experts'. Some of the people to whom I spoke were not too troubled by the adverse criticism which the 'professionals' made about Crossroads, preferring their own opinions.

DH   What do you think when you read about the critics and people moaning about the programme?

M   Well I think that some of those critics moan for moaning's sake, don't you? I've read things up about various things the critics have said have been marvellous, and I've thought it's been tripe. So I mean that's just someone else's opinion, isn't it. I mean I'm not too enthralled about what critics say. I think my own thoughts – if I like it, I look at it.

Others, however, were not happy about the way that critics criticized the programme and also implied in their attacks that the viewers were undiscriminating if they watched Crossroads. Also, they were less happy about other viewers who complained about the programme and they felt that there was enough choice for those people who did not like the programme to watch something else.

w But you've got the choice, haven't you? You either switch on and watch it or you don't.

s I don't think it's right that people should write up and, using Crossroads as an example, say, 'Oh it's a load of rubbish and should be taken off altogether, not just cut down to three days.' If they don't want to watch it they should switch over or off, because there are loads of things that I don't like but I don't write up to the TV people and say that it should be took off altogether, because I know that other people might like it, but what I do is turn off.

One young woman had an interesting observation on those critics who objected to the programme:

J Well I don't think the people who criticize it find it's good viewing because it's too near to their own sort of lives. It's not entertaining watching real-life situations. When they want to be entertained they want to see something different from like everyday life and it's too realistic in a way to be entertaining for them . . . It's too close to home.

DH I wonder when men criticize it and say it's rubbish and all that. I mean, it occurs to me that if it was such rubbish then why do they make such a fuss about women watching it?

J They don't like it 'cos it's sometimes sentimental.

DH And you think women like it for that reason?

J Yes, because men are not supposed to show their emotions and feelings and so if they watch Crossroads and something comes on like Glenda and Kath talking, then they think it's just stupid and unrealistic because they are not brought up to accept emotional situations.

DH So you think it is more a programme that women like?

J Yes, it is, I think. I don't know any men who watch it.

DH I know some but certainly not many. But not only do they – I mean not watch it, but some of them are really quite hostile to their wives watching it.

The feeling that they are watching something which is supposed to be 'not very good' in critical terms, leads some women to feel almost guilty and apologetic that they watch the programme and they excuse themselves for liking something which is treated in such a derogatory way by critics and sometimes by their own husbands.

Watching television is part of the everyday life of viewers. It is not, as is sometimes suggested, a separate activity undertaken in perfect quiet in comfortable surroundings. Nor is it done in a darkened room, as so many programmes are shown when viewed in professional settings like broadcasting or media conferences. Nor is it watched on a video recorder for close analysis of shots, camera angles, or 'messages' in the text, both verbal and visual, as in academic studies. At least, it is none of these things for women with families and husbands to look after and especially it is not the way that they can watch television programmes transmitted in the so-called 'tea-time' slot. Yet it is ironic that many of the programmes which women viewers most enjoy and indeed those programmes which are specifically directed towards them are shown in this period of frantic activity in their daily lives. Crossroads is such a programme. Its transmission times have been discussed elsewhere but to understand the way that the viewers will change their domestic routines to enable them to watch the programme is to go some way towards understanding the appeal which the programme has for its audience.

The comments at the beginning of this chapter were typical of statements which women made about the way that they had altered their meal time in the ATV region when the programme had been moved back from 6.30 to 6.05. The domestic responsibilities of women mean that they are not able to watch with complete freedom and they have to change round meal times and negotiate with their husbands in order to watch the programmes which they enjoy. For most programmes which are transmitted between 5.00 and 7.00 pm this is not a problem. Children can watch their programmes while their mother is moving in and out of the room between the kitchen and the room where the television is located, and when news and news magazine programmes are on they are either ignored or watched spasmodically as their format allows. One young woman, Jane, describes Crossroads and its relation to 'tea-time' viewing:

J   Well, it's easy to watch. It's not relaxing but it's not something that's, like, tense. I mean, you follow the stories but you are not sort of keyed up about it. It's sort of tea-time viewing but not in the sense that you would usually use tea-time viewing, do you know what I mean?

DH   What do you mean when you say, 'Not in the sense you would normally use tea-time viewing'? How would you normally use it then?

J   Well people have got to stop and watch Crossroads 'cos it's on at tea time but with other things you are like rushing around getting the tea and talking and it's sort of in the background.

DH   So you would never have it on in the background? You would always stop and watch it?

J   No, you couldn't follow it.

Ideally, all the Crossroads fans would like to be able to stop and watch all the programme but for many this is an impossible luxury. One of the interesting aspects of watching television *with* the audience is to be part of the atmosphere of watching a programme with families and to see that the viewing situation is very different for different people. To watch a programme at meal time with the mother of young children is an entirely different experience from watching with a seventy-two-year-old widow whose day is largely structured around television programmes. Family situations change both the ability to view with any form of concentration and also the perspective which the audience have on a programme. Marjory, an elderly widow, intertwined household duties with the television programmes, but because she was only responsible for herself she could determine when she worked and how much she watched. She told me: 'I've had it on since the one o'clock news. I turned it off 'cos I was at a bit of a difficult part with the cardigan.' (Her knitting.) Her independent mind was revealed in her attitude to visitors and also showed the regard with which she held soap opera:

If anybody comes here I say, 'Well, if you don't mind, I like to see Crossroads, I'm going to have it on.' Or when Coronation Street comes on, I say, 'Well, if you don't mind,' and I have it on. But I don't keep viewing to interfere with company, really, but I don't think it hurts anybody for half an hour to sit, do you?

Not that she forced her visitors to watch everything on television. As she explained:

> Yes, I watch everything, I never switch off. I don't view so much on a Friday 'cos I have a friend down. We see one or two things and that's it. We see Tarbuck and that's all.

She did tell me, however, that if someone were coming and she wanted specially to watch a programme, she was not averse to telling a 'white lie' and saying she was going out.

Watching with Marjory was a unique experience for me. She was, of course, expecting me to call and she had had her tea and we were able to sit and watch in a state of relaxation and comfort not afforded to many other women with whom I viewed. She served cups of tea in between the early evening news programmes and we sat down without any distractions to watch through from 5.45 until after 8 o'clock. Crossroads was part of the flow of programmes, and as it was a Wednesday evening, we also had Coronation Street to look forward to and were able to talk at leisure about the programmes without any interruptions. ATV Today, as if on cue, also ran a feature about Noele Gordon, because the viewing coincided with the period when the star had just been sacked, and the interrelation of news of the actress and the discussion about the programme in general was an interesting experience.

In sharp contrast to the calm of a widow's small living-room was the experience of sitting in a kitchen/dining area of a modern house. I should point out that although *I* was sitting, the woman with whom I had gone to watch the programme was serving the evening meal, feeding her five- and three-year-old daughters and attempting to watch the programme on the black and white television situated on top of the freezer opposite to the kitchen table. Although I was sitting watching the programme, young children have no respect for the sanctity of media researchers and their need to be undisturbed in the research situation! To them I was as much a target for their attentions as was their mother. I became a part of the shared experience of viewing in that situation and struggled to concentrate against the same odds as their mother. The three-year-old invited me to help her eat her tea, the five-year-old to look at drawings from play school and talk about new shoes in the same manner that they talked to their mother. Mercifully, the tape recorder remains undistracted by everyday life and in the transcription of the interview afterwards the whole situation was recaptured for me. Reliving the experience was not purely nostalgic, for it revealed that points of the story which had been missed by the mother coincided with points on the tape when the children had been at their most demanding, and showed that repetition is necessary in programmes to allow for any points missed by the viewers. However, women with young children do have ways of coping with them and half-watching/half-listening to television programmes at the same time. Listening is the operative word. In this sense, the storyline has to be carried by the verbal level and cannot always rely on the visuals augmenting the story. The woman discussed above, Diane, explained her way of watching Crossroads:

DH In general then, do you watch it regularly?

D   Yes – I miss the odd one or two, I don't always, actually – well, I don't sit and watch it. I'm usually pithering about, but I listen to it. I know what's going on. I think I prefer to listen rather than watch.

DH So you rarely actually go in there and watch it?

D   No, I never watch it in there. Just an odd time if somebody looks as if they've got something interesting on, I go in to see what colour it is. Or if there was something like a wedding I suppose, a sort of occasion, when it would be a bit out of the ordinary, then I'd probably go and see what they were all wearing and . . . but normally I just pither about in here.

DH So, I assume as you watch it then you quite like it, or is it that that's what you have on?

D   Yes I do really, because Monday and Friday I have Nationwide on, but the rest of the time I put that on, and I quite often turn over afterwards.

Clearly, even though she cannot give the programme her full attention, she is not watching it automatically, since she changes

to BBC after Crossroads finishes and on the days when it is not
transmitted. The comment 'I'd probably go and see what they
were all wearing . . .' is an interesting one, as it pinpoints one of
the attractions of television programmes for women and was the
cause of 'leaping between rooms' to view in colour in other houses
where I viewed.

When I arrived at the house of Sheila, she and her twelve- and
sixteen-year-old daughters had finished tea and were hurriedly
washing up in the kitchen at five past six, in order to watch
Crossroads in colour. For Sheila and her daughters domestic responsibilities were more of a problem because they all admitted
to being 'news fanatics', and she in particular had even more
difficulty in fitting in serving the evening meal, washing up and
watching television. Admittedly, as she explains at the opening
of this chapter, she had moved her tea time forward to enable
her to watch Crossroads, but this presented a problem for watching national and ATV news. Even on the news, some items simply
cannot be watched in black and white:

> s   No, I watch it all in colour. And as I was saying to you
>   tonight when you first come, I don't know if you'd seen
>   that at the tail end just before it started, on the News,
>   Prince Charles had been best man at his friend's wedding,
>   his grandmother and Lady Diana was with him, like, and
>   we was in here. Then, like, you know, Tracy and I both
>   obviously had the same idea, I dived in here, 'What colour's
>   she got on?'
> j   Yeah, but half the time I don't watch it. It's on and I can
>   hear it going on because I'm actually dishing out as it
>   starts.

Fashion has a great appeal, whether worn by the stars of
Crossroads or the royal family, and the simultaneous 'dive into
the other room' by Sheila and her twelve-year-old daughter reveals their shared interest in what either 'stars' are wearing. The
incident was a nice example of negotiating and fitting in work
and pleasure, but it also shows how difficult it is to be free to
view uninterruptedly for many women viewers. Janet, Sheila's
sister, who came round to watch with us and talk about the pro-

gramme, echoed the sentiments of many of the women with young families to whom I spoke; she was only able to *listen* to most of the programme because she explained her husband was not so amenable to her changing the tea-time around.

Tea-time and early evening programmes are scheduled to 'catch the audience', and certainly Crossroads achieves that aim for the ITV channels, and it manages this feat against all the odds in respect of the audience. The choice which viewers have to make is not only between the offerings on the other two channels but also, crucially, between other duties, responsibilities and interests which they may have. Television can compete with other interests but not with the duties and responsibilities, particularly those of women towards their families. Yet despite all these restraints, Crossroads maintains and holds its audience.

The notion that people watch a television programme simply because it is on the screen at a certain time does not stand up to serious examination. If viewers watched a screen regardless of the programme, there would be many more programmes with high audience ratings. To suggest, as I have been told by some professional programme-makers, that viewers would watch a blank screen is an insult both to the viewers and to all programme-makers. However, I *have* been told by viewers that they feel that one of the reasons why they watch Crossroads is 'habit'. But what do they mean by this? It is not necessarily a derogatory or negative statement, rather it should be seen in relation to the notion of 'habit' and 'routines'. The regular scheduling of programmes which are transmitted at the same time means that those programmes become part of a certain 'time band' in people's lives. If you have to get the tea every evening at a certain time, put your children to bed, and watch a television programme, then the routine or habit includes the watching of that television programme. However, this does not mean that you only watch it because it has become a habit, in fact women have told me that they wish that the time could be changed so that they would be able to watch without inconvenience of the other duties that they have to perform. For some women viewers this time never arrives, for they never feel free from domestic responsibilities. Some have told me that later on in the evening, if they really want to watch a programme, they do the ironing at the same time because then they are not interrupted. Also, although they may use the word 'habit', it is sometimes expressed as a term of excusing themselves for something which they may feel they *should not* be doing. Some women have been quite self-critical when they have said, 'If I haven't finished the washing up I leave it until after Crossroads.' Of course, it must be realized that television companies do set out to *create* the *habit* of viewing at a certain time. The fixing of certain blocks of the schedule is to catch the audience and fix the viewing 'habit' in the hope of holding the audience for the evening.

One of the most obvious narrative ways that Crossroads maintains the viewing habit in its audience is the 'stop shot' – the last shot after the credits, which holds the suspense over until the next episode. The need to know what happens next helps to create and sustain the habit of watching any programme, but with Crossroads the whole structure of ending with a stop shot is designed to remind the audience what happened before the credits and persuade them to want to see what happens next. The hook of seriality even carries the audience when they do not think the programme is going through a particularly strong period:

DH   Well why do you watch it then?
D   Well I think it's 'cos I've always got to know what's happening in it, whatever the particular situation is. I like to know what's coming next and how it all ends up. No matter how stupid it might be, I still want to know all the ins and outs of it and how it finishes up.

Sometimes women need habits and routines to get them through the day. Another woman, Anne, talked about her interest in Crossroads, before the transmission time changed. She lived on the ninth floor of a high-rise block of flats and had a six-month-old baby:

A   Yes, in between half-five and eight that's my busiest time. Feed him, change him, sometimes bath him – I don't bath him very often. I get Richard's dinner and I always clean up straight away, the washing up, and then I get everything settled and that takes me up to about eight o'clock, 'cos I stop at half-past six to watch Crossroads. And then from eight onwards I just sit and watch the box.

DH Why do you like Crossroads?

A Just that you like to know what's going to happen next, you know. I mean they're terrible actors, I know that, and I just see through that, you know. I just, now and then I think, 'Oh my God, that's silly,' you know, but it's not the acting I'm interested in, it's what's going on. I suppose I'm nosey . . .

Why should she think that she is nosey because she wants to know what is going to happen in a television serial? The answer lies in other comments about why she watches series and serials on television. She said it was 'something to look forward to the next day'. When she was talking about how she spent her time during the day this woman told me that she often looked out of the window of her ninth-storey flat and counted cars as they travelled along the main road below. If you are so isolated that you resort to counting cars, the importance of a television serial to 'look forward to', even when it is less than perfect, does not seem so strange, and 'being nosey' about fictional characters can compensate, however inadequately, for your lack of contact with neighbours or friends of your own.

Habit or routine, the attraction remains. Another woman, Linda, explained:

DH You say you've always watched it. Well, why do you watch it?

L Why do I watch it? Difficult to answer. I've watched it that long that I suppose it's become a routine in a way. (. . .) I mean, for some people who watch it, particularly elderly people, it's all real and it's all happening. Well in no way do I watch it in that light, but at the same time I've watched it that long you tend to think that you, I mean, I don't know them, but you tend to think that you know them. Do you know what I mean? They're familiar.

The combination of the 'time' habit created and fostered by the scheduling coupled with the feeling of familiarity with the characters is a powerful attraction for viewers who become interested in the serial. For even when they are critical of the programme, they are still interested enough to watch.

DH   So if there's a story that you do think is stupid, you're conscious that you think that's a stupid story, but you watch it . . .

D   I'm listening and watching and thinking 'what a load of rubbish', but I still carry on, to see if it's going to get any worse.

Suspense, habit and familiarity are all contributory factors in why the audience watch Crossroads.

What is going to happen next, or the continuous story form, is the mode of soap opera. The storylines and the narrative structure of the serial is the main hook for the audience. They will excuse any faults in acting or production, or even weaknesses in the scripts, as long as the stories continue. There is no particularly deep or complex set of reasons why these stories hold the viewers – it can be explained away by the sheer joy of 'listening to stories' or watching them. It is, after all, the stuff of all drama and literature, and the oral tradition existed long before the written word. Soap operas 'work' at the simple level of telling stories.

There is also, however, the notion that a television programme should be entertaining and this is one which the audience finds very important.

L   I enjoy it ninety per cent of the time, yes, I enjoy it and they become – I can't say they become friends because they don't. They just feel as if you know them. (. . .)

P   But what do you want from a television programme?

L   Not a lot, it entertains me.

When Linda says, 'Not a lot, it entertains me,' she is underestimating the praise which she is bestowing on a programme which achieves that end. To entertain their audience is the aim of all programme-makers and even those who seek to inform and educate know that they need to be entertaining in the widest sense of the word if their audience is to stay with them. Cross-roads undoubtedly does entertain its viewers but it informs them at the same time, for contrary to the widely-held opinions on the nature of soap operas, they are not pure escapism and their audiences are not seeking to escape from their problems by inhabiting a fantasy world even for a brief period. This may be an element of the appeal but it is far outweighed by an engagement with the programme and the problems of the characters, relating them to the viewers' own lives. What the audience find entertaining and why they like Crossroads are difficult questions to answer because there are so many different reasons and answers. What follows is a very broad outline of the main reasons why the people with whom I watched told me that they liked the programme and in some cases why they did not like certain aspects of the programme. The themes are general and the comments are specific to Crossroads, but there are many aspects of them which women have talked about in relation to other programmes I have watched with them and they give many clues to the appeal of this area of programming for women viewers. Of course, Crossroads does have male viewers too, but the proportion is much smaller and although I watched with families, often, when the programme had finished, the women and I moved into the kitchen to talk.

The most obvious question I asked the viewers when I went out to watch the programme with them was 'Why do you watch Crossroads?' The immediate answers were similar to Linda's comment above, but if pushed on why they liked and watched the programme, the viewers did begin to examine their own reasons. Jane was a sixteen-year-old girl who was in the middle of her 'O' levels when we watched the programme together. She was perceptive and articulate about the way she saw the programme:

J   Well they are sort of close to Birmingham people. You can make the connection between Crossroads and your life. I'm not saying our lives are like Crossroads, but it's nearer than Coronation Street and it's, I don't know – it's sort of not common, but unassuming, I think. (. . .) I think Diane's good 'cos she's sort of an all-rounder, if you know what I mean. She gets a lot of different situations and you can see how she copes with them and the problems.

DH   But do you think that the situations they get into and how they cope with them is why people might like it?

J   Yes, because they are down to earth situations, not like Dallas. I mean, deals of fifty million falling through and all that . . . People watch Dallas, I think, because it's over the top, and people watch Crossroads because it's down to earth and things that are sort of in between and in the middle aren't interesting because they are neither here nor there.

DH   Do you think then that Crossroads is actually more realistic than Coronation Street?

J   No, they are about the same. Coronation Street is really set about Manchester and that area, as we know. But Crossroads is − it's real to the Midlands. It is. Not the themes, but the people who are in it. They are like Midlands people. You couldn't say they were from up north even if they had accents, but it's not like them. They don't behave − the characters are just Midlands characters.

Apart from providing strong ammunition against the critics who claim that it does not represent the local region, Jane's statement about Crossroads encapsulates the specific nature of the programme and the way it relates to the lives of its viewers. She also makes a comment which I feel is especially significant in explaining the appeal of the programme when she says that it is 'unassuming'. By unassuming she is referring not only to the subject of the series but also to the quality of the production. What she is saying is that it does not present a glamourized image of life either in its content or in its production style, and this is not meant as a criticism. She also reveals how viewers watch a programme like Crossroads for one kind of appeal and expect an entirely different type of production and content when they watch a programme like Dallas. Viewers bring expectations to a programme which are determined by their knowledge of that programme and its genre and they do not make hostile comparisons across other programme types. As Jane explained:

> Crossroads is different from anything else on telly, isn't it.
> There is nothing like Crossroads on telly so I suppose you
> would have to judge it with the other things not connected
> with Crossroads because there isn't anything connected with
> Crossroads.

However, they do watch the programmes for the same basic interest in the stories and the problems of the characters involved.

No one made any comments of a direct technical nature when
talking about the programme except for one young woman who
watched an episode with me where a deliberate shot had been
included by the director, Mike, for dramatic effect. Benny was
supposed to be coming round from his eye operation and the
shot was from his point of view, looking at Mrs Mortimer, as he
opened his eyes. It began blurred and then came into focus.
Obviously the different shots are noticeable to the audience, and
scenes which Mike had also directed in previous episodes were
mentioned. The women thought the episode was a particularly
good one.

W   Well none of it was boring. There weren't any boring
    bits in it. It was more realistic.
DH What part was realistic?
W   The kitchen was good. The kitchen scene and, er, Benny.
DH In the hospital?
W   Yes.
DH Did you notice things like the out of focus bit with his
    eyes?
W   Yeah, that was good. (. . .) They've been doing more of
    that lately, different sort of camera things. When they
    had Kate on, when they had all the song on and every-
    thing and you could see her doing her gig, they did all
    different shots and that. I didn't think that was Cross-
    roads, actually.

It seems, then, that whereas the audience do not make comments
of a direct technical nature, at least some of them do notice when
extra care and effort has been put in an episode.

The themes which the audience identified as being of most

interest to them revolved around elements of the family – characters, narratives or 'storylines' – and particularly the idea that the programme was 'true to life'. This is perhaps one of the areas where the fans and the critics disagree most about the appeal and qualities of Crossroads. One viewer, Marjory, told me:

M   I like family stories and things like that. I like something with a story.

DH   So do you think that's the reason that you like it?

M   Yes, because it continues, and personally I think it's a lot like real life.

DH   In what way?

M   Well, I mean Jill had her ups and downs, didn't she, and so did Meg, and whatsit with her kiddie who she wants from America, I mean that can happen in real life, can't it. To me it's things in there that can happen in real life. It's not fiction to me. To me it's a real family story.

DH   Now, when you say that, you don't mean you think they're real, do you?

M   No, they portray that and they do it well. It's like we used to have in the pictures in the olden days, we used to have those kind of family stories in the pictures, but you never get them now. You see now, I like that kind of thing. Well, of course, possibly I'm old fashioned, but I still like them.

Clearly, Marjory is under no illusions and is fully aware that the programme is a fiction. She identifies the fact that the incidents in Crossroads *can* happen in 'real life' and *do* happen – if not to her, then to other people whom she may know or know of. It is the difference between the 'possible' and the 'fantastic' which is one of the criteria by which the audience judge fiction for its relationship to their conception of reality.

The production policy of including social problems in the series greatly contributes to the viewers' perception of the reality of events in Crossroads. Since the problems which they introduce do actually exist they are another way in which the audience can see that the serial is based on reality. However, they are well aware when the programme is including a 'social message', although they do not find it intrusive in their enjoyment of the fiction. One of the most important elements in the inclusion of social problems in Crossroads is that the audience do find it acceptable and they do not reject the messages. It is perhaps because the social problems are always related to a character within the serial and not introduced in an abstract way that they do seem to have an impact with the audience. The relation between such issues as reported in news programmes and their impact in the series is one which is important, and in the following extract two women, Sheila and June, discussed why they thought that issues had more effect in Crossroads than in a news programme:

DH   When it's brought in, the mugging thing, what do you think when they bring that in? Do you think they are bringing it in to get a message over or just as an everyday thing?

S   Oh, I'd say it's definitely to get a message over, to try to make people realize to check and all this business like, you know. Because you don't realize how typical of real life . . . You've seen Benny put one of these latch locks up and it's the sort of thing you do do, isn't it. You put it on after like. It is the sort of thing you do do in real life. You never think you are going to be the one who's mugged or burgled or anything like that.

DH   So do you think it has more effect if you saw it on a programme like that than if you saw it in something like ATV Today about somebody being mugged?

S   It might just come over more on a programme like that because this is it. In ATV Today – I always say ATV Today is half like the news. You expect – I mean this is everyday news isn't it, muggings and murders and all this, that and the other. You expect to see that sort of thing on the news and as I said before, I think ATV Today is a great programme, I do, but to me it is a bit like the news. You do get everything and therefore it probably would come over better in – you expect it in ATV Today. But you don't expect it in Crossroads.

J   I think so. For older people, people of Miss Luke's age. They relate themselves with her like, you know.

s   I think you get a lot of old people as well who do watch
Crossroads and Coronation Street, whereas they are
probably sick to death of the news on ATV Today because of the fact that it is all murders and muggings and
that, and it would certainly come over to their age more
in this programme. Certainly it would come over more to
them, you know the older age group, especially women
living by themselves as well, which there is an awful lot
of nowadays as well.

Their argument that it is the unexpectedness of the events
which happen within the serial is an interesting one. It seems
from this perspective that the events which are reported within
news programmes are so predictable that they cease to have such
a strong effect on the audience. Sheila is implying that such
events can be seen to be part of the 'genre of news'. News contains muggings and murders, the audience expects it, it is 'everyday news', but if there is a mugging in Crossroads then it is so
unexpected in terms of what happens in the serial that it has a
more dramatic effect and causes the audience to relate the incident to their own lives or the lives of other people whom they
know. The combination of the familiarity of the characters with
the unexpectedness of the events carries the 'message' more
effectively than the same incidents happening to someone of
whom the audience knows nothing, and which is reported and
expected in a news programme.

The basis of soap opera is its characters and their continuing
stories. When the viewers say, 'I want to see what happens next,'
it is what happens to the characters that interests them. What
happens next? How will she get out of this problem? Will she
meet someone rich, handsome, sexy? Will her children be all
right? Storylines in soap opera are not arbitrary, they are stories
which deal with everyday life and its 'ups and downs', problems
and pleasures; the inclusion of personal, moral and emotional
matters is an integral part of the genre.

'What happened in Crossroads last night?' or more familiarly,
'What happened to Jill last night?' No one has to explain which
Jill is being talked about because the shared knowledge of the
characters which is held by the viewers becomes part of the cul-

tural capital which they exchange in normal conversation. In short digression, I once sat on a train returning from London to Birmingham when British Rail were running their £1.00 tickets during the winter of 1980. Four pensioners sat at a table next to me, complete with their sandwiches and flasks of coffee, and they talked together about many topics of mutual interest. The conversation moved to exchanges about their respective children and grandchildren and names were mentioned. Suddenly, without comment one of the women said, 'What about Emily's trouble with Arthur, what do you think about it all?' (This is not remembered verbatim.) The conversation continued about the mess that Emily was in now that it had been found that he was already married, and how it had seemed too good to be true for her to have found someone like him. How would she be, and how would it all end? As swiftly as the topic had arisen, it switched back to talking about other topics. The uninitiated or 'culturally deprived' would be forgiven for not realizing that the troubles of poor Emily and the misery which Arthur had brought to her were not the problems of the children or relatives of two of the speakers. However, anyone who was aware of the current storyline of the soap opera Coronation Street would have known instantly that it was the fate of the fictional characters which were being discussed. Yet from the conversation it was obvious that the speakers were playing a game with the serial. They did not actually believe that the characters existed; they were simply sharing a fantastic interest in the characters outside the serial. How many of us can honestly admit not to having done that ourselves? How many were not saddened at the fate of 'the beautiful young Sebastian' as he visibly declined before our eyes in Brideshead Revisited during this winter? It is a false critical elitism to allow the 'belief' and enjoyment in a fictional character in one programme and deny others the right to that belief or enjoyment in another.

Similarly, the knowledge which television viewers have about events within the programmes is a form of cultural capital which excludes those who do not watch the programmes. It is actually fun to talk about the characters in a soap opera, and yet the game that viewers play with one another is interpreted as some form of psychological disorder, when for the most part they are well aware that the game is going on.

It would be wrong, however, to create the idea that fans of Crossroads are uncritical of the programme. In fact, the contrary is true, and the viewers possess a level of knowledge about the storylines, the sets and the characters which few professional critics would be able to match. Their positive commitment to the programme does mean that when they make critical remarks their comments are more likely to be of a constructive nature rather than the blanket dismissive mode of some criticism. Their criticism is usually accompanied by a suggestion for improvement and they are unlikely to make comments which would be damaging to the programme as a whole.

Since the storylines are what holds the audience to Crossroads, it is not surprising that this is the area where they have most criticism to offer. However, they do not criticize the stories *per se*, but treat them rather benevolently, waiting to see how they will develop. Generally it is not the theme of any story which annoys them or fails to hold their interest; in fact their willingness to accept a wide variety of storylines would appear to be a *carte blanche* for producers. It is, however, in the length of time which a story runs which they sometimes find rather boring.

An example of the acceptance of a storyline which might have been seen as rather too fantastic by critics of the programme was discussed by the viewers when I was talking about the programme. Briefly the storyline was as follows:

Alison was a young girl who lived with her uncle who was the tenant of Stonebank Farm. He was an extremely religious and bigotted man and she was born before her mother and father were married. Her parents both died and her uncle had brought her up. The fantasy element in the story began with a scar on her face, which her uncle had brought her up to believe was a punishment for the sins of her mother. She had been forced into a completely isolated and protected life and it was only when she began to have contact with the motel through the character Benny, who lived and worked at the cottage, that she began to meet the women characters who inhabit the serial. To condense, she eventually has an operation, paid for by Benny, which removes the scar from her face. She is encouraged and supported in her struggle with her uncle by Miss Luke and other women characters. Her adventures continue with an initial unsuitable love interest and then she goes to work at the Coachhouse for Barbara and David Hunter, and there encounters Hunter's morally unscrupulous son, Chris. In one of the most unlikely sexual liaisons ever seen in a soap opera, Chris stays the night at his father's cottage and takes Alison to bed with him. To be fair, it is possible to see the attraction which Chris would have for Alison, and her hesitant compliance to his seduction was credible; less credible, unless the motive was sheer sexual appetite or the seduction of a virgin, was the attraction which Alison would have had for Chris. The inevitable happened and Alison found herself pregnant, abandoned by Chris and left with the problem of whether to have her baby and try to bring it up herself, or whether to have an abortion. Here the programme introduced an interesting story which enabled an exploration of the possibilities for abortion, and managed to give information about the possibilities for obtaining an abortion as well as including arguments for and against such action. In the event, the character Alison decided that she would not have an abortion and this decision was, in the words of the producer, 'true to the character'. However, the magical solution was employed that Alison eventually had a miscarriage. After this the story crawled along through guilt and religious encounters with nuns until eventually both Alison and her uncle left the series, she to train as a nurse.

The attraction of Chris won through to the women I spoke to. They did not like him but they could certainly see his attraction, especially to Alison. Less likely was the belief that she would have married Benny, which was also suggested in the storyline.

DH What did you think of the Alison story?

W   That was interesting but it went on far too long in the end and we was all saying this, you know, comparing it with your friends and saying, 'Oh, but it's getting on my nerves now.' It's dragging on far too long. And to think that, you know, that she would ever have done anything with Benny was just absolutely ridiculous.

DH Well did you think it was likely that she would have done anything with Chris Hunter then?

W   No, not really. I don't think so personally, no. Because I couldn't tell you Tracey's word on record for him. As Tracey says, he's a bastard, but as I say, he's a lovable bastard. He gets away with it, doesn't he. In my opinion, if he's like that in real life, he could get away with blue murder. You can't help but like him.

The audience were remarkably tolerant about the story. But they did find their patience wearing thin towards the end, not because of the content but because of an unlikely storyline which also went on too long.

The viewers' criticism was often accompanied by suggestions for improvements. These were sometimes at the level of more interesting storylines which could develop the characters whom the viewers liked but thought could be more interesting. The character of Kath Brownlow was one who was particularly mentioned. Viewers liked the actress and the character and women were not impressed by the way that she was treated by her husband,

DH   Which characters do you particularly like or dislike?
L   Well, I dislike Arthur Brownlow, I can't stand him.
DH   And why don't you like him?
L   Because if he was my husband I would have kicked him out years ago – but that is obviously the character, not him. And his wife gets on your nerves, but then again they ought to be able to do something with her part, I think, because she's either laying the table or unlaying it or they are eating. Every time you see their living-room you know there is something on the table. That gets on your nerves.

When I pressed them about how the part could be improved the woman and her husband had different suggestions,

P   Put more meat into it.
L   Yes, she seems sort of downtrodden.
P   Take a lover!
L   Get her husband to lay the table for a change. It's just the character. She's probably doing a very good acting job.

The suggestion from the man is of a jokey nature, but the woman has identified one of the significant characteristics of Kath, who is written as an example of the ordinary, respectable working-class/lower-middle-class woman. She appears downtrodden and accepts Arthur's chauvinism, but not without a certain amount of eyebrow raising at his behaviour. The character as portrayed by the actress is seen as 'realistic', but what the viewers are asking for are stronger storylines so that the character can develop. Other women who talked about Kath have suggested that although the characterization might have been realistic when Kath was at home and without financial independence, now that she has returned to work, part-time in the motel kitchen, she would have gained more confidence and would not take Arthur's attitude and behaviour so readily. These women were often speaking from their own experiences of returning to work and they wished that Kath at least would be allowed to do something to establish her own independence.

The constant referencing of the events within the programme with ideas of what would be likely to happen in their own experience is the overriding way in which the viewers interact with the stories. They also have a remarkable amount of knowledge of what has happened in the serial and make judgements about it, always based in 'real life'. Sometimes these are at a small or trivial level, at others they are much more complex judgements. One woman commented that it was about time that Kath Brownlow had a new three-piece suite because the one which she had was getting to look old, and she added the comment, 'She will be able to when she's having the digs money off Kevin.' This comment was made at a lighthearted level but it did indicate that the viewer was questioning the realism of the serial. She knew that a woman of Kath's class would not be content with the old three-piece suite which the production tolerated. It was a nice example of the realism in the woman's experience being in conflict with the reality of the budget which constrained the production from buying Kath a new suite.

The knowledge of the way women react to stress in their own lives coloured the reactions that the viewers had to storylines within the serial. Stories about Jill's problems and her ways of coping with them were very interesting to the viewers. But they were not totally sympathetic to her reactions to her problems:

> I thought it was quite nitty gritty when – I'm going back a bit
> though – when Jill had that baby by Hugh Mortimer's son. I
> can't remember who he is now but I thought that was very
> good.

Another woman had no such problems with her memory, and
told me stories from the serial in great detail, combined with a
sharp critical assessment of the actions in the story, which were
firmly rooted in her own assessments of everyday life:

> I thought when Jill was going through this drunken phase, you
> know, not so long ago, after this other fella ditched her, I
> thought was pathetic actually. Because she's been through it
> all before. It's about time she . . . you know. It is, it's part of
> life. We could all turn to the bottle but you just don't, do you,
> in real life like, you know. Some do. I agree some do, and I
> suppose that this is what they are trying to get over, that some
> do turn to the bottle. But there again, from the type of family
> that she's supposed to belong to, you wouldn't imagine that
> she would.

The woman was certainly not tolerant towards Jill. The fact
that the character had been through many problems in her life
meant in the eyes of this woman that she should have learned to
cope with them better, and her class position should have stopped
her from taking such a course. Even though there were areas of
Jill's life of which the woman had no direct experience, there
were assumptions about behaviour which were based on ideas
which were common to all women of all classes. 'We could all
turn to the bottle, but you just don't, do you, in real life,' but
then again, 'some do,' so the authenticity of the serial is confirmed. Again, it shows that the actual stories are not criticized;
it is the way that the characters react in the stories which determine whether the viewers will accept the 'true to life' aspects
of the programme.

The idea that viewers 'escape' into a programme like Crossroads is clearly invalid, or at least it is not escapism in the conventional sense of the word. Escapism suggests that someone is
running away from their problems and seeking diversions, even

if momentarily. There are, of course, programmes which do provide escapism for the audience, but soap operas are definitely not in this category. They are precisely a way of understanding and coping with problems which are recognized as 'shared' by other women, both in the programme and in 'real life'. Differences in class or material possessions seem to be transcended in the realization that there are problems in everyday life which are common to all women and their families.

> It brings in every aspect of life, the poorer part and the rest, like Coronation Street as well. It does involve people getting drunk, having babies without being married and all this, that and the other. It is an everyday programme, you get involved in it. I mean, they have brought mugging into it now, haven't they. I think it's because they bring everything into it that it is so good.

One way to understand the appeal of Crossroads for its viewers is through the solutions to the problems or resolutions in fictional terms. In a series like Crossroads the solutions to problems are not obviously progressive and never revolutionary. The resolution to a difficult problem is sometimes achieved by some magical solution disguised as 'natural causes', sometimes helped along by other characters in the serial, and it is rare for resolutions to move outside the consensus. Indeed, Jack Barton stated quite definitely that it was not his aim to move outside the consensus in the treatment of his storylines. However, although not revolutionary, sometimes the solutions can allow the status quo to be shaken up a little and maybe moved on a fraction. In fact, in soap opera much of the dramatic tension is achieved through the dynamics of the changing relationships and situations of the characters. Although the solutions to problems may not be seen as progressive, it is often in the raising of those problems in fictional forms that is important. The problems of facing an unwanted pregnancy and how to deal with it as explored in the storyline with Alison referred to above provided a clue to why the ending was unimportant compared with the issues raised within the context of the story. From the perspective of a radical analysis the fortuitous miscarriage may be seen as a 'cop out', but in dramatic terms, the character, because of her sheltered life and intensively religious upbringing, would have been unlikely to have agreed to an abortion. However, the understanding of the situation and the responses which the raising of the problems elicit from the audience made the fictional resolutions almost irrelevant. For audiences recognize the restrictions imposed on the programme by its time schedule, but appreciate that it is portraying issues which they see as part of everyday life, therefore they can fill in their own understanding of the unseen events in the programme. An example of this was given when I asked one young woman whether she felt that the programme raised issues and then skirted around them.

DH Do you think it could handle things even more explicitly than it does?

J   No.

DH Why not?

J   It's not right. It wouldn't go with Crossroads. It's sort of set its own standard and if it was sort of getting into things too deeply that it shouldn't — well, not that it shouldn't — it wouldn't come across. It would be too scandalous. I mean it might create a bigger audience but I think it would lose some of its appeal.

DH So you don't mind when it's sort of handling something but skirting round it, you think that's all right.

J   Yes, well you can make your own conclusions and guess what they are trying to put across anyway so —

DH So things like, I mean when Alison slept with Chris, you didn't actually see anything —

J   No, but you knew. You knew. I mean it's not that they are not telling you anything, 'cos you know anyway. You can guess what's going to happen, what's going on. So you still get the story without them having to show it.

Unlikely and unsuitable romances abound in soap operas, as indeed in life. In the serial the unlikely ones are usually occasioned by developing a romantic situation between already existing characters who, until the storyline begins, would not seem to have much in common between them for a romantic development. These stories usually have to be resolved amicably by a cooling-off period when the actor and actress are not appearing in the programme, and they can go away to 'get over it'. If the characters are to remain in the serial, they can return to the scene in a new storyline after a period away. Unsuitable romances are much more interesting and they usually develop between characters who are brought into the serial specifically to create romantic liaisons for an established character. The short-term nature of the contracts means that they can either be written out when the storyline is resolved or engaged for further storylines if the character proves particularly successful.

One totally unsuitable romantic interest story developed during the time that I was watching the production and transmission of the programme. It concerned Diane Hunter, the waitress at the motel, and I will let one of the viewers tell the story of the much married and romanced Diane:

W   The first one she married – she had the baby. It's an illegitimate baby, isn't it? She wasn't married when she had the baby. And then she married Vince, to give Nicky a father. Well they were together for a few years, weren't they. Well it was supposed to be a few years and then she married Chris for money reasons.

In the current storyline Diane is 'pretending' to be in love with an American lawyer who is attempting to get her son back from Diane's first husband in America. Diane feels that if she is married to an American she is more likely to get custody from the American courts. The following discussion is between Sheila and June, the two sisters with whom I watched the programme. Both are themselves mothers.

DH   What do you think about this part with her and this American lawyer?

S   Oh she's just going to make a hash of things, isn't she.

DH   If she marries him it will be just another disastrous marriage.

J   But then again, she's doing it for her own means.

S   She's doing it 'cos she wants her child back. She's not doing it for him, is she.

DH   And do you think that's realistic, that she would do that?

J   Ooh yes. Personally I think you would do it yourself.

S   Ooh yes, you would, you know. You imagine having your child taken off you. I think she sees him too often for her status, like, but naturally you would want to go and see him, even at the other side of the world, as often as you possibly could. But if you'd got a chance to get him back you'd take that chance, no matter what, if you was a true mother, like.

J   Especially her, 'cos she doesn't think nothing of marriage, does she, so it's second nature for her to try and use it. It'll be her third marriage now.

I think this is a wonderful example of the supremacy of the audience's own perception of the reality of the programme. It is so firmly based in the women's own feelings of what they might do in the same situation as Diane. It also shows the scriptwriters' accurate reflection of the audience's opinion.

Sometimes storylines are touchstones for experiences which the viewers have and which they see reflected in the serial. One such incident brought home to me the futility of trying to estimate which stories would appeal to which sections of the audience. Marjory, an elderly widow with whom I watched the programme, continually surprised me throughout my time with her. The episode which we watched contained the storyline of Glenda's supposed frigidity and inability to have sexual intercourse with Kevin after they had returned from honeymoon. The sexual aspects of the story were not made explicit in any way and it was at one level a story where I felt one section of the audience might want the programme to go into more detail, yet I would have expected, from the image of older viewers which is prevalent, that someone like Marjory may not have liked this particular storyline. I was proved to be completely mistaken in my speculation and again the incident revealed the intricate workings of the audience with the themes presented in the series.

DH   What do you think about the way the programme sometimes brings in subjects that are a bit difficult, like this story with Glenda at the moment? What do you think when it brings those kind of stories in?

M   Oh well, that kind of thing, her married life is not satisfactory, is it! That's the answer to that. Well, I'm going to say something to you. I never thought mine was when I was young. So I can understand how she felt, and it's rather a worry to you. In other words, well of course in my day they were terribly innocent, weren't they. We didn't really know what was what and what wasn't. And I think we were all a bit frightened. Well I said tonight, you never felt you could really let yourself go, you were frightened of having a kid, and all that kind of thing. Well I can understand that, you see. Now *that* is a thing, when I'm listening to that, I think, 'I can remember I used to be a bit like that.' So that is what I mean to say, whatever they put in Crossroads, it's appertaining to something what could happen in life. It doesn't seem fiction to me.

DH   No, no, that's interesting, because you think if any age group were going to think 'why have they bothered to have that story in,' it would be somebody older, and yet you understood it.

M   It comes to my age group. We used to say we were frightened of our husbands putting their trousers on the bedrail. You know, we had no pill, we had nothing. I mean, I'm speaking perfectly open to you, we were terrified really, if the man got anything out of it it's right, but you were too frightened to let yourself go, and that's just it.

Clearly, if a programme like Crossroads can transcend age to such an extent and evoke in one viewer the memories of her own early married life fifty years previously, it is making connections with its viewers which begin to indicate the importance of the genre. Crossroads viewers contribute to their own understanding of the programme and make their own readings of what the production sets out to communicate. They work with the text and add their own experiences and opinions to the stories in the programme.

It seems that the myth of the passive viewer is about to be shattered. They do not sit there watching and taking it all in without any mental activity or creativity. It seems that they expect to contribute to the production which they are watching and bring their own knowledge to augment the text. Stories which seem almost too fantastic for an everyday serial are transformed through a sympathetic audience reading whereby they strip the storyline to the idea behind it and construct an understanding on the skeleton that is left.

Popular fiction *should* connect with life and reality, indeed it is meaningless if it does not achieve this end, for fiction has always grown from experiences in life. Crossroads connects with its viewers. To look at a programme like Crossroads and criticize it on the basis of conventional literary/media analysis is obstinately to refuse to understand the relationship which it has with its audience. A television programme is a three part development – the production process, the programme, and the understanding of that programme by the audience or consumer – and it is false and elitist criticism to ignore what any member of the audience thinks or feels about a programme. Crossroads is a form of popular art and far from writing it off as rubbish we should be looking at what its popularity tells us about all programmes and indeed all forms of popular art. To try to say what Crossroads means to its audience is impossible for there is no single Crossroads, there are as many different Crossroads as there are viewers. Tonight twelve million, tomorrow thirteen million; with thirteen million possible understandings of the programme. Lew Grade is reported as saying, 'I don't make programmes for critics – I make programmes for the viewers.' His sentiments should be taken further, for in fact the viewers are the critics. Or at least, the only ones who should count.

CHAPTER 7

Whose Programme is it Anyway?

DH   How do you feel about taking out a character that you
have asked –

CD*   – many people to love? Well, obviously, deeply sorry if
there are people in the country – and I know that there
are – who so value a fictional character on television that
their lives are as affected, as they claim to be, by her
removal. The fact that they know as well as I do that that
woman playing the role is continuing to exist and hasn't
been assassinated by the controller of programmes is
neither here nor there. They are writing to me in terms
of contempt, as the murderer of one of their friends. So
I mean, a little puzzling, a little bewildering really, but
expected.

I think Meg should stay, to the people of the midlands she as
come to be regarded as at the least a friend and in some cases
family. I see no reason to dismiss her, why should some face-
less ATV executive have the power over the millions who enjoy
the character she as developed, their is no harm in a piece of
make believe O.K. the critics crucify the series but it is enjoyed
by an awful lot of people especially the old folk and Meg is
the figurehead of the programme and to get rid of her would
signal the end of the show which is the reason I suspect behind
the decision. No leave Meg alone let her continue to entertain
the people who have come to idolize her, away with the back-
room bureaucrats who have they ever entertained?
                        Reader's letter to *Birmingham Evening Mail*

When Noele Gordon was sacked from Crossroads, the *Birmingham Evening Mail*, among others, asked its readers to vote in a
poll saying whether they thought that the actress should stay or
go. At the same time, they asked for letters of not more than 150
words telling why the readers voted as they did. In the words of

---

* Charles Denton, Director of Programmes, ATV/Central.

the television editor, Clem Lewis, 'the response was overwhelming.' The newspaper printed a selection of the letters and the result of the poll which was 2,958 to 250 in favour of the actress staying in the serial.

Reading through the letters gave interesting insights into the way that the audience felt about this specific incident and their affection and empathy with the actress and the character whom she portrayed. They also revealed much about their attitudes to the power of broadcasting institutions and the television companies and their ability to control the programmes which the audience is able to watch. Although most of the anger was directed towards Charles Denton, it is fair to say that he was accused of decisions and actions which were sometimes outside his control and he was specifically attacked for reducing the number of episodes from four to three in 1980, an action from which he must, of course, be completely exonerated, and the blame taken by the IBA. However, the decision to move the serial from 6.35 to 6.05 which had been taken early in 1981 was also criticized, and this was a definite scheduling decision by Charles Denton.

The majority of viewers never feel moved to write to a television company to praise or criticize the programmes or decisions which affect those programmes. Neither do they write in such large numbers to newspapers about a single topic. The experience of reading these letters was one which I found very moving and slightly disturbing. In contrast with the pleasure of watching Crossroads with viewers, 'sharing a laugh', this was a sobering and thought-provoking experience. If this book has an overriding aim it is to argue for the importance of the television audience and the need for their perspective to be considered in relation to the programmes which they wish to watch. The letters which I read contained such overwhelming evidence of their involvement with Crossroads that it would be difficult not to recognize the importance of the programme to them. I make no apology for the mixture of emotions and analysis which pervades this chapter, for it is necessary if it is to reflect the tone of the letters and present a picture of sections of the audience about whom we know very little.

The letters were from men and women of all ages but they

were predominantly from middle-aged or elderly women, many of whom signed themselves 'Pensioner aged 74', etc. The addresses were from all parts of Birmingham and the West Midlands, but again they were predominantly from areas which are classified as mainly working class, although there was a sprinkling of letters from more middle-class areas. Some gave no address, others gave no salutation. Writing paper was varied, with a minute percentage of headed notepaper or 'good quality' paper, but the largest proportion was cheaper in quality; some letters were on paper torn from exercise books or notepads, some on scraps of paper cut up from old greetings cards. By far the largest percentage was on cheap lined paper. The writing was often that of elderly people; many referred to their age but the handwriting also gave clues to their age. While not claiming a scientific analysis of the letters based on their appearance and style of handwriting, when taken together with the facts which the writers stated about themselves, they indicated the class and educational background of the writers – and they were predominantly working class. Certainly a few were much more articulate and these contained the same arguments. I make these observations about the letters because they form part of the evidence I use in an argument which I will be making about this particular section of the television audience and their lack of 'power' over their choice of television programmes. Few if any of these people who wrote letters to the newspaper would attend a public meeting where the IBA asked the audience for their opinions on the programmes provided by the local independent television company, and yet they are a large proportion of the ITV audience. What they reveal in these letters tells much more about their lives, as well as their opinions of the television programmes and the power of broadcasting institutions, as the following example illustrates:

It is a real treat for so many pensioners and housebound folk.

Surely 15 million people cannot be wrong, we enjoy 'Crossroads'. I know that the viewers are mostly women, and that a lot of men scoff at the programme, but I don't think one person has the right to outvote 15 million people.

The men who have sacked Noele Gordon should be sacked

and ladies have their jobs looks as if they only want to please men like themselves no thought for the OAP's like myself 77.

When I first obtained the letters I simply sat down and read them through. I then re-read them and attempted a rough classification along the lines of 'pro the actress', 'pro the programme', 'anti the actress and the programme', and 'letters which contained interesting comments on themes other than simply referring to the actress'. It soon became obvious that my categories were to be pitifully inadequate, because the letters embraced far more points of view than I had originally gleaned from reading them. I then began noting down points which were made in the letters and these soon numbered over fifty separate points, which showed the large and varied amount of interest which the viewers had in the programme.

The main theme in the letters was, of course, to support the actress Noele Gordon, and to praise her both as a performer and a person. A précis of the contents of many letters would read, 'Noele Gordon is Crossroads.' None of the letters confused reality and fiction, but they did consider both the actress and the character.

I think it is absolutely disgusting and very sad indeed to hear that 'Meg' Miss Gordon is to be dropped from Crossroads. I'm a senior citizen and in my view and all my friends Crossroads may as well get off the air it will never be the same again and many faithful viewers will I'm certain not watch it any more. Meg is a lovely lady and showed a good many actresses on TV what charm and good manners are all about which is very much lacking in the world today.

Many letters incorporated the belief that if Meg were to be removed from the programme, Crossroads would not survive.

If Meg goes, why carry on with Crossroads, I for one will never watch it again, because Meg is Crossroads.
Yours hopefully,

I just want to say that Meg Mortimer must not be sacked. (What an insult) to a lady that has put 17 years of Good Watching. Why should she go and no explanation. All my neighbours agree. She must not go. I am a pensioner and love Crossroads.

At a personal level, in relation to the actress, many of the letters were shocked at the treatment which she had received by being sacked by ATV after her long association with the company. Many of the viewers had watched her in Lunch Box, the live lunchtime programme which she had hostessed, and had watched Crossroads since it began. They felt that she had been badly treated as an employee by ATV. Many said that they would not watch the programme when she had left. A few identified the advertisers as the only people whom they thought had any real power with the television companies and suggested that the advertisers should withdraw their advertisements in support of the viewers who were also their customers! A combination of viewers and advertisers would indeed provide an effective power to change the views of independent broadcasters. Such a powerful liaison is unlikely, however, since the spending power of the elderly is extremely limited and not likely to gain the support of the advertisers.

There was a marked feeling that the action of Charles Denton in sacking Noele Gordon might have been a deliberate ploy to hasten a planned demise of the serial. Some identified the qualities of the character, which they saw as most positive, as being a reason for her not leaving the serial.

I think it would be a disaster to see the departure of Noele Gordon from Crossroads. I can't understand why, she is to my mind the figure head of the programme and everything is built around her, and I for one do not want to see the character of the programme changed.

Ironically, it was precisely because the character was too dominant in the series and that she was the figurehead against which it was felt that it would be impossible to develop different storylines, which was instrumental in the decision that she should leave the cast in the interests of the programme developing along new lines. The division of interests and opinions between the television company and its viewers is nicely illustrated in this letter.

There is no question but that the idea of the Crossroads family, as a family who have become 'friends' to the viewers, is the predominant way that the performers in the serial are seen by the viewers. Working with ideas of the family and family life as the norm to which it is desirable to strive, the representation of family life in Crossroads is one of the main features to which the audience responds. It is the qualities of the characters in relation to accepted ideas of feminine, domestic, or – in the case of Meg – motherly behaviour which they find attractive. The following letter extract gives clues to the appeal which the character has for the audience:

> The serial depicts a kind of steady life we would all like to see today. Meg Richardson the kind of woman we would all like to be. Quick, steady as a rock to everyone in an emergency. Motherly enough to comfort people in trouble and a happy person to laugh with any funny situation and firmly to be committed to family life and keeping families together. Finally, why should these television people tell us, what they think we like.
>
> Mrs P, aged 71.

The qualities of good, capable Meg, with her ability to cope with all the problems of women's lives, are the qualities which are seen as positive by many women who, throughout their own lives, have conformed to the ideas of women's position in family life. Those qualities portrayed as positive virtues are a confirmation to women that *they* have been pursuing the 'right goals' in their own lives. For television not only provides models for us all, it also confirms those models through characters portrayed in its programmes. The model provided by Meg Richardson is seen as positive by the women in the audience because for the major part of her life she has managed to bring up her children and run a successful business without a husband. Husbands and suitors have come and gone but Meg has remained. The importance of the mother and the strength of a positive female image in the programme was emphasized in many of the letters. The empathy which the women feel for the shared characteristics of women characters in the programme is pertinent.

Noele Gordon should quite definitely stay in Crossroads, as Meg Richardson, because she is Crossroads. Without her the whole programme would lose its appeal to the many thousands of women viewers who look upon her as an understanding and helpful Mother!

Surely it is about time that TV Producers considered the women viewers a little more instead of always appearing to consider only male viewers with either Sport or Sex!

Stay! Of course Meg must stay. You don't kill off your friend, your Mom, your Nan.

Come off it gentlemen – leave our Crossroads alone! – and our Coronation Street too! How do you think they have been at the top of the polls for so long? Because I represent 50% of our population – good, honest, English wives and mothers. Leave Crossroads alone! And Meg – and Diane and Doris Luke – yes, even Benny. They are our friends . . .

The idea that the company was breaking up a family was seen as an extremely undesirable action, and many letters suggested solutions for the programme-makers which would leave the family intact. Jill could marry Adam and they could manage the motel while Meg had a long holiday: this was a common theme. Letters which expressed the sentiments, 'Don't break up a happy family,' were in abundant evidence and again in this context there was an interesting combination of reality and fiction. The actor, Roger Tonge, who had played Sandy in Crossroads died on 25 February, 1981 and many of the viewers mentioned his death in their letters, expressing the sentiment that it had been sad enough when he had died and the character had to be 'lost' from the series. To cause unnecessary upsets by another 'death' in fictitious form in the series would be too disturbing for the viewers.

The loss of a character from a long-running series has no real parallels in other fictional forms. By their domestic nature and their presence as part of people's everyday lives, going into their homes, the serials and the characters within them give the viewers the feeling that they 'know' them. What is seen as the indiscriminate removal of a character by production decisions is not seen as acceptable by the audience. In this sense events in a long-running series seem to have a different basis for the audience from other fictional forms. A character in a novel may die, yet the book can be re-read and the character can 're-live' for the reader. Similarly, a character in a film may die, but films are often seen many times by their ardent fans and in any case, a character in a film is usually enclosed within the one film and the audience has not built up a long acquaintance with them. Radio and television create characters which are slightly different from the stars in films. Because of the everyday nature of many characters, they are not felt to be so removed from the audience, and the audience feel able to comment on their fates. Even when a relatively minor character is written out of a serial it causes concern that they will not be seen again. This is always doubly regretted when the actor or actress does not wish to leave the serial. When a major character is written out in this way then it always causes resentment and draws a large audience. There is a long history of this in radio and television series. It could almost be seen as a feature of the genre. Charles Denton identified it:

> It's the Grace Archer syndrome, isn't it. It's setting fire to Grace Archer done as a deliberate move on the part of the BBC on the opening night of ITV to distract attention from the opening night of ITV, which did the job wonderfully.

Crossroads has had twenty-three deaths in the serial since it began. Seventeen of these have been 'fictional deaths', to remove characters from the series, and six have been deaths of the actors or actresses. However, apart from Carlos the chef, and Hugh Mortimer, Meg's husband, the enforced fictional deaths have not been to major or long-running characters. In 1969, the actress Beryl Johnston, who played Kitty Jarvis, Meg's sister, died, and this did remove a strand of the storylines since the original conception of the series had been about the lives of the two sisters. Often, when characters have been written out through a fictional death, the storylines have exploited the death for dramatic impact. In spring 1979, when Linda Welch, played by Lesley Daine, slipped, banged her head and was killed, the series exploited her death in a storyline which involved the wrongful suspicion of Benny as her murderer. The ensuing outcry and defence of Benny, which resulted in 'Benny Is Innocent' stickers and campaigns, was, on one level, an example of the audience joining in with a joke with the television company. However, it did have its serious side and was one of the incidents which highlight that there are some members of the audience who do see the series as not really fiction at all. Kathy Staff, who plays Miss Luke, talked about this aspect of the letters which she receives:

KS   There are people who realize that you are an actress and are doing a job, but then you do get the others that really believe in you as a character and they write to you as Doris Luke. For instance, when, a couple of years ago, Benny was had up – well, the police were looking for Benny for murder and it wasn't Benny at all. Of course it was the manager of the garage that pushed the girl down and then whipped off and Benny came in and found her. And I mean, the letters I got telling me what happened, 'You go, Miss Luke, you go to the police and tell them, I saw it on my television. It wasn't Benny at all.' And I mean they really believed it and they were writing to me as Benny's best friend, and like a mother character, to get him out of trouble.

Interestingly, there was no outcry about the death of the character Linda Welch because she was, in soap-opera terms, a 'bad' character. It seems that the audience do not grieve just for death in soap operas, but for the death of 'good' characters to whom they relate. If the character is 'killed off' in the series, then the audience know that they will not be able to see that character again because, almost alone among television forms, soap operas are not repeated. Unlike novels, films, shorter series, there is no way that the programmes are likely to be seen again. The removal of the character Meg from Crossroads is regretted because the audience feel that the programme controller is depriving them of seeing a character whom they have grown to appreciate and, more importantly, to approve of. It is not simply the removal of the character but also the loss of the qualities embodied in that character which are regretted.

It should also be remembered that many of the people who wrote these letters were themselves, by self-description, elderly and it was the reminder of their own mortality and their identification with the character of Meg Mortimer as their 'friend', which contributed to their plea for her reprieve by the television company.

In the same way that it is impossible to remove a television programme from the social situation and setting of its viewers' everyday lives, it is also impossible to separate the timing of a transmission from the events which are going on in the 'real' world. During the summer of 1981 there were serious social disturbances in major cities in Britain. Beginning in Brixton and spreading through Toxteth in Liverpool, Handsworth in Birmingham, Leeds and many other places, young people, many of them black, seriously disaffected with their arid lives in Britain, where the economic situation left them unemployed, the scapegoats for society's problems, and living in inner cities with specific problems in their relations with the police, showed their feelings about their lives in a way which, for a while, shocked the rest of the country. Television and newspaper coverage of the scenes was intensive and spectacularly dramatic. Commentators painted a picture of devastation and an imminent breakdown in society, and television news coverage was extensive. Imagine the juxtaposing of a domestic serial, Crossroads, with news bulletins containing shocking visual scenes and accompanying commentary – the contrast is intense.

The interaction of the reception of programmes termed fictional with factual or news programmes is a major way of understanding the appeal of soap operas and comedy programmes. Programmes are viewed as a flow of events and viewers do not mentally switch off and forget what has happened in one programme when they view the next one. This is not to say that they confuse the events in factual and fiction programmes, simply that there is a tendency to make comparisons and connections between life as *revealed* in the news programmes and life as it perhaps could be, as *portrayed* in fictional forms.

Not surprisingly, then, there was a marked tendency in the letters to equate the programme with a form of stability in society which the viewers felt was slipping away. They talked about the programme as something which they seemed to see as an 'anchor' in a changing world: 'Give us stability in our lives. We have enough change forced upon us in our lives no more is needed.'

They cited ideas of a consensus of standards of behaviour and sexual morality which they felt were being eroded in society, and suggested that these values were retained in Crossroads, whereas they were dismissed in other programmes.

Don't this new modern writer for Crossroads realize we see enough wrong and trouble in our present day life and are glad to watch something a bit slow. Anyway the younger set have their programmes – Crossroads and Coronation Street are for us who want to see life as we'd like it to be at times.

The letter above illustrates the importance of fantasy in soap opera. It is not only seen as representations of domestic life as viewers experience their own lives, but also a representation which portrays life as they *would like it to be*. As one woman wrote, 'Leave us in peace with our fantasy programmes.' The element of momentary escapism is important to consider, especially in relation to the way that women have talked about news programmes to me. When they have said that they do not watch the news because it is 'depressing', they have also said that they feel helpless in the face of the reality which is represented to them in news programmes. This was not because they do not understand the content, nor because the broadcasters are not getting their message or information across clearly, but rather because the message is all too clear and because it induces in the viewer a feeling of powerlessness and overwhelming despair at the world which they see. In the face of this it is perhaps understandable when some viewers feel that the world of Crossroads is more acceptable than the 'real world' and why they object so strongly at what they see as unnecessary change.

Perhaps the single most surprising aspect of researching and writing this book has been the awareness which it has brought to me about old people and their lives. Quite incidentally, while they wrote letters in support of the actress, they gave information about their own lives and the importance to them of some television programmes. For the letters were often not simply about television but about the way that old people experience their lives and how they feel about their role in society. The following are some examples:

I think the way they have treated Noele Gordon is shocking . . . I have watch her on television for many years also Lunch Box and Stars on Sunday. I know I am old 88 years but I am a good judge of people. All I can say keep going Meg we will miss you.

I live alone and over 70 and look forward to seeing Crossroads. I feel she is a friend come into my home. I do hope that you can do something to save her.

I am an OAP . . .

I am 77 and housebound . . .

Why do people suddenly begin to sign their letters with their age and give social and economic status as 'pensioner'? What are they trying to say about their own self-identity? There was a sense of the writers expressing in these definitions two contradictory feelings – a sense of wanting to say that they had reached a certain age and that their opinions *should* be taken into account, but also an expression of the feeling that they knew that their opinions would *not* be considered, precisely because they were now old.

The responsibility for the elderly in society cannot, of course, be laid solely at the door of television companies, but television can and does appear to provide one of the few pleasures and areas of contact with the world for elderly people. It is ironic that Charles Denton, himself an ex-documentary film-maker, who has supported the production and transmission of some of the most 'socially aware' and disturbing documentaries made for British television, should have upset so many people by his decision to end the fictional character of Meg Mortimer. The new Midland independent television company Central, the successor to ATV, has a deliberate philosophy of letting its viewers know that it 'cares', yet many viewers feel that their wishes are ignored by the television companies. When Charles Denton told me, 'an obsession with unreality does indicate something wrong in your own life,' he was expressing a truism, albeit unintentionally, about the lives of many of his elderly viewers. Television is very important to the elderly and housebound and while the rest of society fails to alleviate the situation for many elderly people who live alone, the entertainment and sense of contact which programmes like Crossroads provide for its viewers are surely among the most valuable aspects of the medium. For there *is* something wrong in the lives of many people and the reassurances which they derive from fictional programmes should not be underestimated. It may be difficult for television companies to accept this area of responsibility, but if this section of their audience is entertained by programmes which they do not themselves rate highly in professional terms, they should begin to question for whom the programmes are made.

It should be disturbing for television companies, both ITV and BBC, to learn from these letters that many of the elderly viewers felt that television programmes in general had little appeal for them. There were many examples of programmes which were not enjoyed and topics which it was felt were in too great an abundance in programmes in general. These could be summarized as 'too much sex and sport'.

> If you want to move anybody, move some of the sports rabble.

> I suggest you take some of the other things off, all for men, such as football, cricket and all the rest and leave Meg alone.

> We are OAPs, this type of entertainment suits us, as we hate and detest violence, murder, raping and heartily sick of seeing people jumping in and out of bed.
> (This letter was signed by ten neighbours whose ages ranged from 65 to 83.)

In contrast, soap operas, including Coronation Street and Emmerdale Farm, were very popular and there is no doubt that the genre of domestic serials has a great appeal to this age group. The notion of the family has been discussed elsewhere, but the predominance of older female characters in the series was also of importance. Specific mention was made of Annie Walker, Hilda Ogden and Elsie Tanner from Granada's Coronation Street, and Annie Sugden from Yorkshire Television's Emmerdale Farm. None of these actresses is young and it is perhaps their continuing attractiveness as they grow older within the serial which appeals to and evokes empathy in the viewers. There are few women characters in this particular age range except in the soap operas and the request not to kill Meg off but to let her 'retire gracefully' was expressed by viewers with a sense of personal involvement with the character. The affection with which the viewers held the programme was expressed in the sentiments of one letter: 'Aren't we entitled to have a little show of our own?'

Some recognized the sincerity of the television controller when he said that he wanted to improve the programme but hastened to reassure him that there was no need for improvement:

> Some people never learn. They gaze into the future searching for someting special – but when they already have it they are too blind to see.

It was, of course, the idea of unnecessary change which disturbed many of the elderly viewers, the thought that they would be losing the familiarity of the character and a reluctance on their part to agree with the idea of the production team that change could be innovative. It was a direct clash of opinions; the viewers did not want change even if it were to be for the better. This, of course, was more than a reaction to the events within the television programme for it was also a reflection of the way that they felt about the changes which were going on around them in their lives and in society as a whole, and over which they felt they had no control.

The letters revealed a very real anger and indignation directed against the programme controller, Charles Denton, and the producer, Jack Barton, but also against the IBA, for their disregard of public opinion in their actions regarding Crossroads.

> Why is it that the TV Planners never do what the majority of the TV Watchers want? They take it off its best time ie 6.30 pm, put it on at 6 pm. Only three episodes per week is shown when we used to have four.

> I really can't understand what gets into these ATV chiefs and programme planners . . . I thought the whole point of television was that viewers should have programmes that they enjoy, but ATV chiefs seem bent on preventing this. Crossroads remains a very popular programme with a great many people enjoying

it. It is consistently in the top viewing lists, yet ATV chiefs want to change it all. Already they have cut it from 4 to 3 nights a week. As if that wasn't bad enough, they now want to remove 'Meg'. Its ludicrous. We *want* 'Crossroads'. We *want* Meg. Let us have what *we* want and what *we* enjoy. We will soon tell you when we are fed up. We shall switch off.

The anger was not solely in respect of the sacking of Noele Gordon but also in response to other decisions which had been taken. There was a recognition that the opinion of the viewers was not considered when decisions involving productions were made, yet there was a genuine lack of understanding about the commercial logic of certain decisions which were made:

Surely the very fact of her popularity and that of the programme is the only fact that counts. Why make changes in the format of a programme which has many many times been proven to please the viewing audience, which I would have thought was the *only* opinion that counts.

The importance of public popularity in preference to the popularity among those in authority was sometimes, quite correctly, directed against the IBA:

I would like to ask IBA who exactly the programmes are made for . . . Crossroads is one of the few decent programmes that viewers obviously want to watch and it is constantly being attacked by IBA . . . Judging from their decisions, the wrong people must be in control at IBA.

and again:

Why should these television people tell us what they think we like. Isn't TV for our entertainment or is it for the convenience of ATV demigods?

Some letters were not without their humorous side:

I always have a feeling that someone has the 'knife' in Crossroads because it is so popular. I didn't like the way they altered the time – that was spiteful because it wasn't such a convenient time and it was one way of decreasing the number of viewers and so they hoped it would become less popular. The television is for public entertainment, not to satisfy the whims of producers – who are very tempremental and awkward human beings.

As well as being staffed by 'awkward and tempremental' people, many of the viewers felt that the television companies were completely out of touch with their own viewers, and what they wanted and liked:

So the controllers of ATV think Crossroads is so old fashioned. Let me tell them that the viewers are old fashioned and like it. Most of the older generation watch this programme, because it is day to day living as we see it.

Some letters were abusive to the controller and many suggested that it was he who should be given the sack rather than the actress:

Whoever, or whatever, is the cause for this decision is obviously out of touch with what the public wants and should resign their position as being representative of viewers' wishes.

In fairness to Charles Denton, it should be said that there were some letters which were in favour of the sacking of Noele Gordon. Again, some were abusive of the actress, some felt it was time that she moved on and, in fact, felt that her career would benefit by working in other programmes, and some agreed with the decision that had been taken, seeing it as beneficial to Crossroads:

I would like to congratulate the ATV Chiefs responsible for deciding on a new format for Crossroads and for their brave decision to exclude Miss Gordon.

It is a brave decision! because they must have realized some viewers would take it as a personal rebuff – in view of the fact that some people actually *believe* Crossroads exists.

As a male viewer, I found Miss Gordon very professional, *but* she seemed to always 'over' act her part – and consequently a somewhat childish soap opera became truly amateurish.

Television programmes are made by their creators, producers and performers, but a programme only really exists as a process of communication when it is watched or 'consumed' by the audience. Producers and the audience may differ about the content of a programme, but 'ownership' of a programme does not normally become a subject of conflict between the production team or broadcasting institutions and the audience. Crossroads during this period became the subject of an argument which appeared to be about the 'rights of possession' between the television company and the audience. There would seem to be something in the nature of a long-running serial like Crossroads which causes its fans to feel that the programme belongs to them and makes them extremely resentful when the television companies and the IBA make changes to the programme with which they do not agree.

Television companies play a contradictory game with their viewers. They deliberately create an illusion of possession through the use of language, talking to their viewers about 'your television company', 'your programmes', 'your evening's entertainment on ITV'. Can they blame the viewers for then believing that the television company and the programmes have something to do with them? Viewers insist on talking about 'our Meg', 'our Crossroads', 'our soap operas', 'our programmes', and tell the television controller, 'Don't tell us what we like!' There is in these comments a suggestion of a sense of collective possession of this popular entertainment which does not exist in relation to many other programmes. It is hard to imagine any collective possessiveness about News at Ten, or even a single dramatic play – although individual newscasters and performers do elicit the same response from the audience.

What has been evident from the response which ATV's controller received after his action in sacking Noele Gordon is that it becomes difficult for the creators to make changes in the format or content of popular programmes and that the question of their 'right' to make changes with which the audience does not agree is one which is questionable in the eyes of the audience. Charles Denton made his decision on professional grounds but it was taken almost as a personal affront by the viewers. He saw the necessity of keeping the freedom of the creators to make the decisions involved in the series. When I questioned his right to destroy the fiction he had asked viewers to believe in, his reply was rooted firmly in the production camp:

Are you asking the creators of it to suspend their disbelief as well and to believe that it is part of their own daily lives, because if you are, you are asking for the extraordinary things that happen.

In the first two days after he had sacked Noele Gordon, when he was in the firing line of public outcry against his actions, Charles Denton described the viewers' letters to him as 'ranging from abuse to threats':

They've gone over the line in believing in it as a serial on television and they believe that a part of their lives – in many cases, a realer part of their lives than their own domestic circumstances – is being removed from them by the act of somebody who is in control of them.

For him, the series is fiction and the decision was a professional one which he saw ultimately for the benefit of viewers since his concern was to improve the serial:

Now this actually is a professional decision, to do with the future of Crossroads and how to develop Crossroads in the future. And my belief, and others associated with it believe that it cannot satisfactorily be developed without removing that central lynchpin of Meg Mortimer. I believe she has to go for the serial to be developed at all, and that's the only reason, professional judgement.

He denied wanting to finish the serial or to reduce its popularity.

DH Things that you said about the programme would lead me to think that you are not really thinking of axing it, which is what people are saying.

CD It's because I am thinking of continuing it that the change has to happen. I mean, it's my judgement, not personal at all on her, but professional on the serial and shared by its producer, that the development which we hope will revitalize it – as you say it's moribund – but revitalize it in our eyes as well as the more general audience can't take place with her there. The character is so much a part of the way the thing is that the thing will continue to be in its present pattern if she continues there.

DH   Why does it never then change if she's not in it anyway?

CD   Well that's where I get a little bit worried because I have to use kind of awful incomplete arguments. She is a living presence in it. Plot lines revolve around the character whether she's there or not.

Charles Denton also wanted the serial to contain 'stronger writing', and to 'just bring it slightly nearer my concept of reality'. There is no doubt but that he thought that he was acting both in the interests of his viewers and the television company. If the serial were to remain it required changes which would 'revitalize' it and carry it through into the new era which was coming to the company. But which company? For it should not be forgotten that at the end of the year when the actress was due to leave the serial, there were changes ahead for the television company holding the Midlands franchise. On 1 January, 1982 ATV ceased to hold the franchise for the region and Central took over as the new holder. New programmes were planned for a new company with a new image. If Crossroads were to remain, it needed changes or improvements which would not run the new company into skirmishes with the IBA such as had occurred with ATV. Hidden in the words 'production decision' are the interests of the new company which was to be taking over, and the ultimate interests of his staff as well as the audience who were to watch the programmes.

CHAPTER 8

Crossroads in Crisis – Crossed Cultures?

DH   Does Crossroads actually catch the audience, does it do what it sets out to do?

DG*   Well, it does. I think that programmes like Crossroads do play a very important role as part of the scheduling. I mean it is important to have recognizable parts of the schedule where people know they're going to get something which is predictable, I mean in the sense that they know the kind of programme they are getting. It has familiar characters in it and so on, just as a weekly quiz show has in a sense the same kind of qualities, whether it's Larry Grayson and Isla St Clair in the Generation Game, or Bruce Forsyth doing Play Your Cards Right, and in a purely commercial, audience-gathering sense it's important also to have programmes that can deliver an audience with some degree of regularity. But in Britain, at any rate, those considerations are not the only ones.

It may seem surprising that a programme which has achieved what it set out to should have been the subject of so much controversy and criticism. But it must be remembered the areas from whence the criticism emanated. The IBA, the government-appointed watchdog of the independent television companies, is the official voice which has made the most publicly audible criticism of Crossroads. But there has been much more criticism, sometimes audible but at other times unheard, which has had an equally insidious effect on the programme. These criticisms have come from various areas: the press, the broadcasting industry, many from within ATV. Jokes are made about it by comedians both on television and in variety performances at

* David Glencross, Deputy Director of Television, Independent Broadcasting Authority.

theatres. Of course, there is nothing wrong with joking about a programme — it is a form of recognition — but the jokes which are made about Crossroads are usually at a level which is at best unkind and crass and at worst cruel and vicious. No one seems to make gentle jokes about Crossroads; cheap jibes are more the vogue. There has built up over the years a tradition of 'knocking Crossroads' and it is difficult for the programme to escape this image. Many of those who knock the programme do not actually watch, and whereas some programmes have become cults, there is a cult of not watching or liking Crossroads.

Within the broadcasting companies there is a feeling against Crossroads which I learned of before I ever began the work for this book. One director at the BBC, who has made some of the best popular television series, brought Crossroads into the conversation when I was interviewing him and praising some of his programmes as ones which women had told me that they thought were good. He said:

> What sadly takes the gilt off the gingerbread from my point of view is that they probably watch Crossroads, which I dismiss as being professionally inept. So it doesn't actually alter my opinion of what I do. If they also take notice and watch Crossroads, that slightly removes any influence or any feeling of responsibility I have towards them. That's the understatement of the year. I mean if it only takes that to influence their lives then they are obviously influenced by all sorts of things that happen to touch their lives. If they want to watch Crossroads, that's fine. I have no argument against the principle of Crossroads. My argument against Crossroads as a professional is that it is so inept that the people who make it should actually have their tickets revoked permanently.

In that extract he manages to dismiss the programme, the programme-makers and the audience in one fell swoop, and all of it was completely unsolicited in respect of Crossroads.

Within ATV there were people who spoke to me who had very similar opinions about the programme. Some worked on the programme, others worked within the company, but their opinions were part of the atmosphere in which the programme-makers had to operate. One person who was professionally extremely

competent and who actually had worked on the programme was
unequivocal in total condemnation of the programme:

> I have felt a bitter resentment at wasting my time working on
> it. I have sat up until midnight doing camera scripts, we've
> worked until as late as possible at Bradford Street, the PA has
> then had an endless job of retyping camera scripts, the lighting
> director has knocked his pan out, or has done for me, we've all
> worked very hard in studio, and the end result is such absolute
> shit that we might as well have adopted the process of, 'I'll do
> the camera scripts on the train from London to Birmingham,
> and let's try and get home by six in the evening.' Because the
> actual quality of the material does not justify any work at all,
> and anyone who puts any work into Crossroads has been
> conned. He's being conned, his professional pride is being
> called into the game, and there just ain't no point in doing
> anything. The show is not worth it, the show does not inspire.

He continued with an onslaught against technical limitations
caused by the lack of production time, the lack of quality in the
scripts, and the miscasting within the roles, although I should
add that at other points he did say that there were performers in
the serial who were excellent, and his comments were not critical
of the performers as such but rather of miscasting.

x   You get tackiness, profound tackiness.
DH   What do you mean by that?
x   I mean lines badly played because there isn't time to re-
      hearse them, I mean shots not really well executed with
      bad lighting because there isn't time to relight and so on.
      It's just, it's something and nothing now. It's out-
      rageously bad, it's appalling, it's an insult to anyone who
      watches it, because the script is so dreadful. I mean, re-
      gardless of the technical and production values, the two
      basic production values of Crossroads are never met. The
      scripts are abysmal and the casting is by and large abys-
      mal. Now you can get away with one or the other just
      about, but you can't get away with both. If I was a pro-
      ducer, scripts like that would never pass my desk. Anyone
      with just the slightest ability to judge a script would

bounce those scripts straight back and either get the writer to do better, which they may be capable of, or have new writers.

At a technical level he was not critical of the staff's standards of work, but of the company's overall policy which had led to the lack of practice in the drama area:

I mean the company I suppose by definition have created a climate from which very little drama gets done. So I think by and large the sort of work that normally comes out, unless highly motivated, is of a fairly low standard. It's largely because of lack of practice. You see, you get the minuses of bad design and I think by and large very bad lighting, with what is both a minus and a plus – cameramen who are desperately eager to please but don't actually have the experience to know when enough is enough, who therefore frame every shot perfectly, you know, with the lamp foreground and the light streaming through the window in the background. And of course the knack is actually to strike a balance where you shoot things perfectly without making you aware of shooting them. So I think for those reasons, oh and the final reason that one is so aware of the visual effect of Crossroads, if you are looking at it critically, is because the scripts are so abysmal that directors desperately try to make it look pretty.

The problem for the crews at ATV Birmingham has always been that the more prestigious productions have been made at Elstree studios. When Central's new studios are complete at Nottingham and Margaret Matheson, Central's new head of drama, brings her own plans into operation, there should be much more opportunity for drama productions in the Central area. With those new developments it would be a pity if Crossroads remained the poor relation while other forms of drama were allowed to progress and enjoy more facilities.

One of the ways to understand the reluctance which the directors have in feeling positive towards a programme like Crossroads, which, despite its popularity, has no critical standing within the broadcasting industry, is to understand their relationship with the programme from the point of view of their career. There is a constant judging of output within the industry and people within television do talk about programmes which they have seen the night before. However, they are not usually simply judging the programme, but judging their fellow workers who made the programme. This is confirmed by many people to whom I have spoken all over the television industry, and is, of course, a quite natural situation. Another director who had worked on Crossroads put it very honestly:

> Crews don't judge you about what you're like as a director, they judge you by the show you're scheduled to do. I mean, I tend to judge people by the shows they're given to do, and I know, since I'm about to be for the first time in the position of being producer, hiring directors, as opposed to producing and directing, that I will be actually choosing directors to do a show – that I wouldn't judge a guy by what I necessarily believed to be his worth, because I don't know what his worth is. I would judge him by what he's done before. And crews do exactly the same.

Although they are aware that they make programmes for their audience, professionals within television want critical acclaim not from that audience but from their fellow professionals. Mike Holgate and I went through a long discussion about what he felt about directing Crossroads and this reveals clearly the two factors which are in process in producing programmes:

> MH You know it's the bone of contention with Crossroads directors that if you try and make it look nice and pretty and you work on it nobody notices, 'cos nobody watches it, nobody who would – well I don't mean nobody . . .
>
> DH Go on, say – nobody who?
>
> MH Well, nobody from the business, nobody who would be critical from the business would watch it, yeah?

The problem for directors on Crossroads is that they know that while they are working on the programme, they may be contributing to its popularity, but no one who has any influence in terms of their own career structure is likely to notice their work. It was clear watching the production schedules and studio work on Crossroads that the amount of effort which had to be put into making Crossroads was equal to the effort which any director whom I had watched had to put into their work. In fact, in many cases it was a considerably greater effort, but there was little work satisfaction to be felt after they had made that effort.

DH   I think that the real contradiction is that supposedly you're having to make programmes for the audience but really, I mean you're not making them for yourself, but it's your work satisfaction that's going into it and it's in that sense . . .

MH   But then you're, as a director, you're a one man audience anyway, aren't you, and you've got to be because you're the only one that can appraise the whole thing, appraise performances, and so therefore you are representative of the twenty million people who are watching it and you are deciding what they will like.

DH   Well how can you ever then be content with something that doesn't content you?

MH   Within a certain framework, yes it does. I'm usually quite happy with what I've done, 'cos I know that I've moulded a script from nothingness into workability and into something that is quite passable and even on occasions quite good and on occasions bloody awful as well.

In fact, the director, and, to a certain extent, everyone who worked on the programme felt that they were sold short in terms of the time and facilities which were given to the programme. I asked Mike how he would defend the programme against its critics from within the broadcasting industry:

MH   But I think we're sold short. The first thing I would say is, 'Hang on a second, I'm getting a bum deal because I'm not being allowed enough time to make this very good.' So the attack would be back inwards at the producer and the controller of the programmes. I would say to them, 'Look, give me more time and give us more money and it would look better, it would look twice as good.' But how do you get that across? Because they all turn round, they'll counter it and say, well it's always been done like that for the last eighteen years and it still looks okay, so how can you defend that? And you can't because you've never been given the chance to do it.

Directors may feel that they are not able to progress in terms of their career, nor are they able to show their abilities on Crossroads, but others in the production team feel more resentment against the company for not recognizing the contribution which the programme has made to the prestige of the company:

> Within the business itself I think we have been badly let down, to be absolutely honest by people within our own company, let alone the industry as a whole. The loyalty hasn't been here within our own company. It was, up to a certain point, but the loyalty isn't there anymore. We are dismissed as a bore and a nuisance because we take up too much studio space. What they don't realize is just how much we've contributed on behalf of the company, for the company, as company people. We've worked our guts out and all we get is a little bit of scorn.

There is little or no prestige in working on Crossroads. The praise comes solely from the producer to his staff and performers and they rarely have any external encouragement or praise. Conversely, they feel the aura of disdain which prevails in relation to the programme, and they feel the icy blasts of control which emanate from the IBA. I asked Maggie French how the production team had felt about the public criticism which it received from the IBA:

DH   When the IBA last year made you swap from four to three episodes what was the reaction to that within the company?

MF   Well, I suppose I can only really talk personally. The effect it had on us as a team was yet again that we were being relegated. One can only try, but I wish at some stage somebody would write, in English, what standards they are actually referring to, because I think the standard is bloody good. What I do think they are trying to do is to compare it with a one-hour production that has probably taken six to twelve months to produce, and then you're in cuckoo land, because you don't even know what you're talking about. You can't do that, that's out of the question. But if they would tell us in English – well, me – I don't know whether Jack's ever been told – in English, I'd like to be told just once . . . I don't mind any changes, even staff, if they want to change the staff, if they think that's what it needs, if somebody will give me one valid reason for it. But those never seem to be forthcoming. It's just 'improve it,' a sweeping statement.

What are the criticisms which the IBA has against Crossroads and why did they insist that the programme was cut from four to three episodes in 1980? I asked David Glencross whether the IBA had had more contact with ATV about Crossroads than they had with other companies:

DG   No, I wouldn't say so, except that it's a programme that's been there for a long time and it occupies a fairly large chunk of the early-evening schedule. So if they moved out of the evening schedule as a whole . . . I mean in a sense one has come to accept Crossroads as something of a fixture, like Coronation Street, but I wouldn't say about the content of the programme itself that there is this enormous thick file of correspondence between the IBA and ATV, not at all.

DH   So when the authority has had things to say, what has it been about in general?

DG   As with all long-running series, Crossroads or anything else, or a quiz show, if a thing has been running for a long time, I think you do ask the question, 'How much life has it got in it?' Not only IBA ask that question, obviously the companies themselves do. In nearly every case the long-running series have been brought to an end by the companies themselves without any prodding from us. The Authority has never suggested that Crossroads should come to an end, but it has raised the question as to whether the number of episodes that ATV were providing each week was the right one. And in the end in April last year that number was reduced from four to three, as you know.

An interesting comment to note in the above is that the question is whether the IBA and the companies feel that there is any life left in the series, and not whether the audience feel that. In fact the audience are pretty quick to show when they do not approve of a popular show, by simply not watching it, and there was no such indication from the audience in relation to Crossroads. If the audience did not think that there was anything wrong with the programme, what did the IBA feel was the problem?

DG   I think we felt, and a lot of people outside the IBA felt also – and when I say people outside the IBA, I don't mean highbrow figures or establishment figures; such people aren't interested in whether Crossroads is on five, four, three or once a week actually – but what we felt at the IBA and what some critics had pointed out was that the production standards were not as high as they might be, and this was in part due, in our view, to the fact that there were four episodes a week. That's a very considerable burden, to script, rehearse and record that amount of TV per week and we felt that if the pressure was eased slightly, purely in a logistical sense, that would give a bit more time and the polish of the programme would be that much better. The argument is often made that if you look at Coronation Street, that's only done twice a week, but we certainly never made any direct comparison when talking to ATV. In any programme there is a relationship between the time you have for preparation and the finished product, so that was the first thing, and the second thing was when you're looking at the overall schedule, the overall service in the week as a whole, as we have to do in terms of reacting, I don't think you can consider any one programme or series of programmes in isolation. You have to try to say, 'Well, taking the output as a whole, how much of particular kinds of programmes should we have?' And we have over the years built up certain expectations and in some cases regulations. We try for instance to have a balance between different kinds of programmes, we limit the amount of . . . for example, we limit the number of feature films that are shown, and

> long TV movies, because we feel that otherwise there
> would be a danger that certainly in peak viewing time
> almost everything else would get squeezed out. So we
> wanted to make a bit more room in the early evening for
> the possibility of other kinds of programmes emerging
> from the company itself.

Two interesting arguments are going on in David Glencross's
comments. The first is related to the production standards of the
programme, which are in turn related to the amount of money
which is spent on it. The second objection which the IBA were
making to the programme is in terms of the genre and its right to
a place in the schedules. In answer to the argument about the
possibilities which the vacant slot opens up for companies to
show other types of programmes, it must be said that there have
hardly been any innovative creations in the vacated slots. They
have mainly been used for re-runs of situation comedies,
extended news programmes or language programmes. It is also
hard to imagine any similar comments being made about news
programmes blocking the schedules, because the consensus, at
least among the institutions, is that news programmes are important. Nevertheless, they are no more important than popular
fiction programmes.

The arguments about the lack of technical facilities given to
Crossroads is clearly a strong one in terms of the production
team's defence when they are attacked for not reaching the
standards which they feel that the IBA require of them.
David Glencross and I discussed the production facilities
which are available to Crossroads, and what is revealed at
the end of the discussion is that Crossroads is suffering
much more as the technical developments in the industry
are made available to other productions, while even the
most basic facilities are denied the production. The IBA are
well aware that the allocation of editing facilities does affect
the finish of a programme, but agreed with the television company that the provision of those facilities would be extraordinarily expensive for a programme which goes out 156 times a
year.

DG   Post-production editing is extraordinarily expensive.

DH   Yes, that was Charles Denton's excuse. He said he couldn't afford to put it on if he gave it that.

DG   Yes, that backs up what we felt here. The fact is the very sophistication of electronic recording, editing, processing has actually increased the time that drama directors want because it can give the kind of flexibility, if you've got the time to do it, that previously was only available with film. So now electronic drama of any kind is proving not to be quicker at all by and large – I'm not thinking of massive things like Brideshead – but electronic drama, electronic production of all kinds, the more the producers and directors want to exploit the techniques that are now available, the more time and the more expensive it becomes. In terms of money and time – I mean time is money, but it's also physical resources in the studio.

DH   When you say time, you mean not just the time of that director, the time using up a particular editing suite, and that editor?

DG   Yes. And the machines, if they're not being used for that, then they'd be used for something else. It's one of those dilemmas and paradoxes. TV production in the late 70s has a greatly increased capacity now. Electronic editing has made directors, not play with it, but use it to its ultimate as it were, and push it as far as they can.

The actual costs of Crossroads are not discussed in this book because costs for television production are extremely high and it is not particularly helpful to know actual amounts which are spent on individual series or programmes unless there are figures available for comparisons across other programmes and types of programmes. What is important to consider is that money provides facilities, and it is in the allocation of facilities that Crossroads fares very badly compared with other programmes. The production team know this, the controller knows and so does the IBA, yet it is rarely mentioned in discussions of the programme. It is a problem which is getting more acute as the electronic facilities become more sophisticated and Crossroads drops further behind in comparison with other programmes. Clare Mulholland, the Midland regional officer with the IBA, discussed the question of the companies and the allocation of funds:

DH I wondered if the IBA said things like, 'Why doesn't that programme have post-production editing?' which does make a difference not just in terms of finish but in terms of how people are working when they are making it.

CM Well, we might say that in informal discussion with companies. We wouldn't lay that down as policy. The company are supposedly the professionals on production standards, although we would offer opinions about the way. That really is their job and it is up to them and their colleagues to decide whether productions are worth transmitting and are as good as they can be. So on the whole we would not be laying down the finer points of what is wrong with a particular programme.

The role of the IBA in relation to the independent television companies is extremely powerful. Its role is defined as:

The IBA is the central body appointed by the Home Secretary to provide Independent Television (ITV) and Independent Local Radio (ILR) services in the United Kingdom. In accordance with the IBA Act, the Authority plans the structure of the Independent Broadcasting system, chooses and appoints the programme companies, supervises the programme planning and advertising, and transmits the services. The Authority's function is not merely regulatory. It is closely involved in all aspects of planning and the formulation of policy and is ultimately responsible for the content and quality of everything transmitted. All major developments are discussed and matters of policy decided at the meetings of the Authority held twice a month, and the Chairman of the Authority keeps in close touch with the day-to-day activities of the system.*

In 1981 the IBA awarded the new franchises to the television companies who had applied to operate within the ITV regions. As part of their public consultation, which included many public meetings and invitations to the public to make their feelings known to the IBA about their local television company, the IBA

* *IBA Television Handbook*, 1980.

also commissioned the British Market Research Bureau Limited to conduct a survey on attitudes to ITV. This was published as *Attitudes to ITV – Report on a National Survey Volume I, Commentary*. It was published in June 1979. The purpose of the research was defined as: 'to examine the attitudes of viewers all over the country towards ITV in general and towards the service they are provided with at a local level in particular . . .' Among the topics investigated in the survey were 'the awareness of individual ITV companies and associations with them'. In answer to the question relating to knowledge of programmes made by their local company, most people in the ATV region *named* Crossroads as the programme which they identified as made by their local company. Similarly when asked to name the *type* of programme most often associated with the local company in each region, the answer given in association with ATV was 'serials' (Crossroads, etc). The research was carried out between 29 January and 7 April, 1979, and it seems incredible that one month after the report was published, the IBA should have publicly criticized ATV for their production of Crossroads, and insisted on the reduction of episodes from four to three. Since their research had shown the popularity of Crossroads, it seems strange that they have appeared to ignore those findings and insisted on the changes. Viewers *do* know and *like* Crossroads, and the constant criticism and attacks cannot be explained away by technical and production inadequacies, because these could be remedied if they were really the only factors involved in the continuing controversy. Why is there so much hostility and animosity against Crossroads? Why does it offend so many people and yet please so many others?

The television profession has never quite come to terms with Crossroads, almost as if they were ashamed of their own creation. It is as if they have wondered at its appeal and secretly wished they could disown it. Crossroads is not alone in suffering this fate, but it is an extreme example in terms of its continued success with its audience despite the attacks made upon it. Time and again writers, producers and performers create successful, popular programmes and then critics within their own industry shy away in horror as the programmes win popular acclaim.

What these critics seem to be saying is that they do not like the programme they themselves make, and, in effect, that they wish the rest of the television audience would not persist in wilfully watching it. But broadcasting institutions cannot continue to see themselves as some sort of *arbiter elegantiae* for all their viewers. The popularity of a programme like Crossroads, despite the unrelenting criticism it attracts, cannot be explained away in terms of differences in professional or personal taste. The programme provokes a straightforward clash of cultures. What the critics are saying is, 'This programme offends me and my cultural values.'

What the fans are saying is: 'I like this programme and, for the most part, it entertains me.' The audience holds sheer entertainment value high on its list of priorities, yet the Reithian legacy of the need for broadcasters to 'educate, inform and entertain' seems to have left programme-makers with an uneasy feeling about the status of entertainment and whose values it should reflect or represent.

Because soap operas are designed to catch their audience they do incorporate features which appeal to that audience. Soap operas are specifically aimed to appeal to women, although women are not their only viewers. It might be suggested that the popularity of the form among women could have contributed towards the contempt in which the genre has been held. Values in soap operas are far removed from heroism or adventure; they are, for the most part, domestic, personal, but they are not trivial and the characters in the serials are often forceful and dynamic. They do connect with the everyday experiences of their audience and the programme-makers successfully communicate their messages. Jack Barton commented on the aims of his programme:

DH How consciously have you brought in what you could term 'social' issues into the programme? Has it been a conscious decision?

JB Yes, because, simply, what you're doing anyway is you're storytelling, and it's like an extended family – your audience – and you're telling stories to people in a sitting-room and everybody loves listening to a story. If, in the course of that storytelling, it is something which is topical, first it has to be entertaining and it also, as long as it's entertaining and good drama, lots of emotion in it, fine, then that's the sugar-coating on the pill. Because here is the hard fact that we're trying to get across, and it doesn't matter what it is, what kind of social comment we're trying to make, they know because it is something that is relevant, and they're wondering how we're going to solve it. Maybe we can give them an answer to it. It's the curiosity again of how other people behave, how they cope with a situation.

However, my research with the audience has revealed that their interest is not simply in finding out how others will cope with a situation and learning from the messages of the programme, but, crucially, also involves their own feelings and thoughts about how situations should be coped with. Communication is by no means a one-way process and the contribution which the audience makes to Crossroads is as important as the messages which the programme-makers put into the programme. In this sense, what the Crossroads audience has revealed is that there can be as many interpretations of a programme as the individual viewers bring to it. There is no overall intrinsic message or meaning in the work, but it comes alive and communicates when the viewers add their own interpretation and understanding to the programme. In criticizing the programme, those who attack it have missed out on the vital aspect of the appeal of the programme for its viewers. It is criticized for its technical or script inadequacies, without seeing that its greatest strength is in its stories and connections with its audience's own experiences. The programme is a form of popular art precisely because it has a relevance for its audience.

Crossroads is not unique, it is not something different from other forms of popular communication, but what it should point out is that there should not be a separation of art from everyday life. Conventional criticism is rooted in the traditions of literary critical theories, which demand that certain arbitrarily-defined standards are imposed on any piece of writing, whether it be a novel, a poem or drama. This form of criticism stems from the idea that a work of art is separated from its audience and should be appreciated for certain qualities contained in the work. It is based on the notion that to understand a work of art you have to have a 'key' to unlock the secrets; these are the tools of critical analysis. This notion has even been turned on its head in relation to Crossroads because the critical attacks on it suggest that its viewers do not have *any* critical faculties precisely *because* they like the programme. This is clearly elitist and nonsensical. What the viewers of Crossroads reveal is that they bring critical faculties which are rooted in everyday experiences and commonsense, and not in some arbitrary critical theories.

Television is a new form of contemporary art and communication; the possibilities for its expansion appear to be endless. If it is to progress and communicate with its audience it should free itself of the forms of criticism which are rooted in other forms of communication. Broadcasters should recognize that when they do attract a large audience they should not despise that audience nor the programmes which most appeal. A soap opera which appeals to and connects with the experiences of fifteen million people is as valid and valuable as a work of art as a single play or documentary which may attract four million viewers. Neither is better nor worse than the other. They are simply different programmes and each is dependent on the understanding which the audience brings to it for its ultimate worth.

A New Motel – A New Future?

Throughout the summer of 1981 the outcry surrounding the impending death of Meg Mortimer continued. The press sought to discover how she would die and Jack Barton threw them titbits but concealed his plans by recording many different endings to confuse and maintain the secret until the actual transmission of the final episode in which she was to appear.

On Wednesday night, 4 November, the eve of Bonfire Night, a furious blaze engulfed one of the most familiar sights on British television, the reception area of the Crossroads Motel. The cliff-hanger which held the viewers in suspense over the weekend was whether Meg had died in the blaze or would be allowed to retire gracefully to distant shores. On Wednesday 11 November the viewers breathed a sigh of relief, for their efforts and pleas had not been ignored. Meg was allowed to sail off happily into the sunset. The change in decision about the character's fate was a direct result of the action by the viewers, and here, in perhaps the most unlikely area of television, the viewers had shown that they do have the power to change decisions.

DH   In the summer Meg was going to be killed, so why did you change your decision through those months?

JB   It changed simply because of the overwhelming response and reaction from the viewers. And it wasn't just the strong protests for a variety of reasons; the ones that really touched me were the ones from the elderly. There were masses of other protests for other reasons, from very physically able people and what it meant to them, it was touching their emotions as well, but the elderly people who lived for nothing else, the lonely and people like that, and it was to them going to be a real bereavement, and it was like losing one of their own, and as I say it was so overwhelming, the response, you couldn't ignore it.

DH   Was it easy to say to Charles, 'I'm not going to kill her,' or not?

JB No, I simply went to Charles and I told him that what you have to accept is the personal involvement and how it is going to affect people's lives. You can't just high-handedly say, 'We'll kill her, and it'll be a smashing funeral,' or whatever. You can't. And he accepted that decision. I said, 'But because I'm going really to go for maximum publicity on it, and we'll really go for this, we'll get both bites of the cherry.' And so purely from a professional point of view and getting the press and the whole nation interested in what might happen that's why until the last minute you didn't know whether she'd live or die. I know my audience, and that is what they wanted, and I can't tell you the mail I've had since. It's like as if you're the home secretary and you've reprieved someone, and they say we're eternally grateful to you and so on.

DH And can you say how you want the serial to be in the future?

JB I think there comes a time, anyway, when you do need to introduce new blood, and I think some of the older ones must gradually be phased out. You have to move with the times, there's no question of that. In a programme that is constantly changing you've got to also remember that there are characters in the programme played by actors who want to get off the treadmill themselves and for a variety of reasons they will either want to get back into the theatre and recharge their batteries or psychologically and mentally they want a rest from it, etc. So we fic-tionally write them out, they come and go, they come and go. And the audience don't mind that because they've got a reason why, they've gone down to nurse old granny for six months or whatever, and they know that they'll be coming back. But in a case when you come to an end of a contract and for whatever other reason Charles may have had, you come to the contractual thing where they're not going to renew an artiste's contract, then I'm left with the problem of trying to write that character out and not make my viewers too unhappy, try to reassure them that life will still go on, etc. But at the same time it made me feel that I cannot allow again that much emphasis to be placed on one character, because it's too much of an upset and it upsets too many viewers too much. So therefore in that sense it has now given us more freedom, it doesn't have to revolve around the one character any longer, we now all need each other that much more as a team. I look forward with great excitement to the future because the old motel itself was getting outdated so we're having a new one built and I look forward with great excitement to that and being a little more efficient in its service and keeping the old faces, but being able to introduce quite a few new ones. I look forward with great confidence to the future.

As this book goes to press the *TV Times* for the week of 20 to 26 February hails 'The new Crossroads Motel rises from the ashes' and begins its copy, 'A new era begins for Crossroads this week, bringing a fresh dimension to television production.' Crossroads viewers will hope that the motel continues and that although they have lost Meg Mortimer, they will not be deprived of the stories of the other characters and their everyday lives, which they find so enjoyable and entertaining.

Index

The figures in the photographs on the backboard are as follows:

1 LYNETTE McMORROUGH – GLENDA BANKS, DAVID MORAN – KEVIN BANKS, PAUL HENRY – BENNY HAWKINS.
2 LYNETTE McMORROUGH – GLENDA BANKS, KATHY STAFF – MISS LUKE, NOELE GORDON – MEG MORTIMER, JANE ROSSINGTON – JILL HARVEY, ANGELA WEBB – IRIS SCOTT.
3 NOELE GORDON – MEG MORTIMER, RONALD ALLEN – DAVID HUNTER, JANE ROSSINGTON – JILL HARVEY, PAUL HENRY – BENNY HAWKINS, ROGER TONGE – SANDY RICHARDSON.